MASTERING VISUAL COMMUNICATION

Tips, Mistakes, and Case Studies

OSMAN KARAKAS

1

About Book

Book Title: Mastering Visual Communication:
Tips, Mistakes, and Case Studies

Type: Digital E-Book

Format: **PDF**

Size: 6X9 inches - 15.24X22.89 cm

Total Pages: **229**
2023

E-mail: okarakas@hotmail.com

Web: www.osmankarakas.com

CONTENTS

Preface

Welcome to "Mastering Visual Communication: Tips, Mistakes, and Case Studies." In today's fast-paced world, where information is constantly bombarding us from all directions, the ability to communicate effectively through visuals has never been more crucial. Whether you're designing a website, creating a presentation, or developing an advertising campaign, your success often hinges on your proficiency in visual communication.

This book is designed to be your comprehensive guide to the world of visual communication. It has been crafted with the aim of assisting students, professionals, and enthusiasts in harnessing the power of visuals to convey messages, tell stories, and engage audiences.

Visual communication is a dynamic and ever-evolving field, and this book reflects that dynamism. It explores fundamental principles of design, common pitfalls to avoid, and practical tips for creating compelling visuals. Through a wide array of real-world case studies spanning advertising, web design, branding, social media, presentations, data visualization, and multimedia, you'll gain insights into how these principles are applied in various contexts.

In the following chapters, we will delve into the art and science of visual communication, dissecting the elements that make visuals not only aesthetically pleasing but also effective in conveying information. You'll discover the importance of simplicity, the psychology of color, the nuances of typography, and the critical role of accessibility in design.

The book also examines the ethics of visual communication, urging readers to consider the ethical implications of their design choices. We'll explore the ever-evolving landscape of technology and its impact on visual communication, including the exciting realm of virtual reality and the imperative of sustainable design.

Throughout this journey, you'll find practical insights, actionable tips, and thought-provoking case studies that bring the concepts to life. Whether you're a seasoned professional looking to enhance your skills or a newcomer eager to grasp the fundamentals, this book is your companion on the path to mastering visual communication.

We invite you to embark on this exploration of the art and science of visual communication. Let these pages be your guide as you discover the power of visuals to inform, persuade, and inspire.

Thank you for choosing "Mastering Visual Communication: Tips, Mistakes, and Case Studies." We hope it becomes a valuable resource in your quest to become a proficient visual communicator.

Sincerely,

Osman Karakas
okarakas@hotmai.com

Chapter 1: Introduction to Visual Communication

Defining Visual Communication

Visual communication is all around us, shaping our perceptions, influencing our decisions, and connecting us with the world. It's a fundamental aspect of human interaction that predates written language. In this section, we'll explore the essence of visual communication and lay the groundwork for our journey into this dynamic field.

What Is Visual Communication?

Visual communication is the process of using visual elements to convey information, ideas, or emotions. It involves the strategic use of images, typography, color, and other design elements to create visuals that effectively communicate a message. These visuals can take many forms, including photographs, illustrations, charts, graphs, diagrams, videos, and more.

At its core, visual communication is about making complex ideas or concepts understandable and memorable. It's a bridge that connects the creator's intent with the audience's understanding. Whether you're designing a logo, creating a poster, or producing an infographic, your goal is to use visuals to tell a story, convey a message, or evoke a response.

The Multifaceted Nature of Visual Communication

Visual communication is a multidisciplinary field that draws from various disciplines, including graphic design, photography, illustration, psychology, and marketing. It's not limited to any one medium or platform, and it plays a vital role in diverse fields such as advertising, web design, branding, journalism, education, and more.

In essence, visual communication is a universal language that transcends cultural and linguistic barriers. It's the reason why a well-designed symbol, like the peace sign or a smiley face, can be instantly recognized and understood worldwide. Visuals have the power to evoke emotions, trigger memories, and convey complex ideas in a fraction of a second.

The Importance of Visual Communication

Visual communication is not merely a decorative aspect of design; it's a strategic tool for effective communication. Here are a few reasons why visual communication is of paramount importance:

1. **Instant Impact**: Visuals grab our attention quickly. In a world where information overload is the norm, well-designed visuals can cut through the clutter and make an instant impression.

2. **Memorability**: People tend to remember visuals better than text. A carefully crafted visual can leave a lasting imprint on the viewer's mind.

3. **Universal Appeal**: Visuals can transcend language barriers, making them accessible to a global audience.

4. **Emotional Connection**: Effective visuals can evoke emotions and create a strong connection between the message and the audience.

5. **Clarity**: Visuals can simplify complex information, making it easier to understand and retain.

In the chapters that follow, we will delve deeper into the principles, techniques, and best practices of visual communication. We'll explore how to harness the power of visuals to tell compelling stories, convey messages with impact, and avoid common mistakes that can hinder effective communication.

Visual communication is both an art and a science, and mastering it requires a combination of creativity, knowledge, and practice. As we journey through this book, you'll gain the skills and insights necessary to become a proficient visual communicator.

In our exploration of visual communication, it's crucial to begin by understanding its significance, historical evolution, and key terminology. These aspects lay the foundation for a comprehensive grasp of this dynamic field.

Importance in Various Fields

Visual communication plays a pivotal role in a wide array of fields, influencing how we perceive, interact with, and understand the world around us. Here's a glimpse into its significance in various domains:

- **Marketing and Advertising**: Visuals are central to advertising campaigns, branding, and marketing strategies. They have the power to make products and services appealing and memorable.

- **Journalism and Media**: Newspapers, magazines, and online publications rely on visuals to complement stories and engage readers. Infographics, photographs, and videos convey information efficiently.

- **Education**: In classrooms and online learning environments, visuals aid in comprehension and retention of information. From textbooks to educational videos, visual communication enhances the learning experience.

- **Entertainment**: Films, television shows, video games, and multimedia experiences are all products of visual communication. They captivate audiences through storytelling and visual effects.

- **Business and Corporate Communication**: Visuals are integral to corporate presentations, annual reports, and internal communication. They make complex data and ideas accessible.

- **Web and User Interface Design**: Websites, apps, and user interfaces rely heavily on visual communication to provide intuitive navigation and a pleasant user experience.

- **Healthcare and Medicine**: Medical illustrations, diagrams, and visual aids help healthcare professionals explain complex concepts to patients and peers.

- **Social and Environmental Causes**: Visuals are powerful tools for advocating social and environmental causes. Posters, documentaries, and social media campaigns raise awareness and inspire action.

Historical Evolution

Visual communication has a rich history dating back to prehistoric cave paintings and ancient hieroglyphics. Over time, it has evolved in response to cultural, technological, and societal changes. Key milestones include the invention of the printing press, the rise of photography, the advent of television, and the digital revolution.

Understanding this evolution provides insights into the role visuals play in shaping human communication.

Key Terminology

Visual communication has its own set of terminology that forms the basis of our discussions throughout this book. Here are some key terms you'll encounter frequently:

- **Visual Elements**: These include images, typography (text), color, shape, and space— essential components of visual communication.

- **Design Principles**: Fundamental guidelines for arranging visual elements effectively, such as balance, contrast, alignment, and hierarchy.

- **Typography**: The art and technique of using typefaces (fonts) to convey written information.

- **Color Theory**: The study of how colors interact and their psychological impact.

- **Visual Hierarchy**: The arrangement of visual elements to guide the viewer's attention and understanding.

- **Composition**: The organization and arrangement of visual elements within a design.

By familiarizing yourself with these terms, you'll be better equipped to navigate the world of visual communication with confidence.

With a solid understanding of the importance, historical context, and key terminology of visual communication, we're now ready to delve deeper into the fundamental principles of visual communication.

Chapter 2: Principles of Visual Design

The Role of Design in Communication

Design is not merely an exercise in aesthetics; it is a powerful and deliberate act of communication. In this chapter, we embark on a journey to uncover the profound significance of design in the realm of visual communication. Design serves as the bridge between creators and their audience, enabling the conveyance of messages, ideas, and emotions with precision and impact.

Design as a Language

Visual design is a language in itself, one that speaks to us through images, typography, color, and arrangement. It transcends the boundaries of written and spoken language, allowing for universal understanding. Just as words are carefully chosen to articulate thoughts, design elements are meticulously crafted to convey meaning. Whether you're crafting a logo, designing a web page, or creating an infographic, your design choices send messages and elicit responses.

The Visual Conversation

Consider design as a conversation between the creator and the viewer. It begins with a message or an idea that the creator wishes to communicate. Design serves as the medium through which this message is transformed into a visual form. It's not merely about making things look attractive; it's about ensuring that every visual element contributes to the clarity and effectiveness of the message.

Strategic Use of Design Elements

To be a proficient visual communicator, one must master the strategic use of design elements. This includes understanding how size, color, typography, and composition influence the viewer's perception. Each design choice is deliberate and guided by the desired impact on the audience. A bold font may convey authority, while a warm color palette might evoke feelings of comfort and familiarity. The arrangement of elements can guide the viewer's eye and emphasize key information.

Emotional Resonance

Design has the remarkable capacity to evoke emotions and create connections. A well-designed image can stir joy, empathy, or nostalgia. The choice of colors can elicit excitement, calmness, or trust. Through design, you have the power to connect with your audience on an emotional level, making your message not only memorable but also deeply felt.

Design Ethics

With great power comes great responsibility. Designers must consider the ethical implications of their work. Design choices can influence opinions and behaviors, for better or worse. It's essential to approach design ethically, avoiding manipulative tactics and ensuring that the message aligns with honesty and integrity.

As we journey through this chapter, we will explore the principles that underpin effective visual design. These principles are the tools in your arsenal, allowing you to create visuals that resonate, engage, and communicate with precision. We'll begin by unraveling the concept of "Visual Hierarchy," which is fundamental to guiding the viewer's attention and understanding.

Visual Hierarchy:

Guiding the Viewer's Attention

In the realm of visual design, achieving clarity and effective communication hinges on the skillful use of visual hierarchy. Visual hierarchy is the art and science of arranging design elements in a way that guides the viewer's attention, conveys importance, and facilitates understanding. It's about orchestrating a visual symphony where every element plays a specific role in the composition.

The Importance of Visual Hierarchy

Consider the following scenario: you're designing a webpage or a poster with a wealth of information to present. Without visual hierarchy, this abundance of content can overwhelm the viewer, causing confusion and frustration. Visual hierarchy comes to the rescue by providing structure and order. It enables the viewer to navigate through the content effortlessly, focusing on what matters most.

Key Elements of Visual Hierarchy

Visual hierarchy relies on a set of design principles and techniques that manipulate various elements, including:

1. **Size**: Larger elements tend to command more attention. By varying the size of elements, you can immediately draw the viewer's eye to the most critical information.

2. **Color**: Bold, contrasting colors can make an element stand out. Whether it's a vibrant call-to-action button or a highlighted heading, color can signify importance.

3. **Typography**: Typeface choices, font sizes, and text styles (such as bold or italics) can create

distinctions between headings, subheadings, and body text.

4. **Whitespace**: Adequate spacing around elements not only enhances readability but also isolates important content, making it more noticeable.

5. **Position**: Elements placed at the top or center of a design often receive more attention. Eye-tracking studies have shown that viewers tend to start scanning from the top-left corner, so important information strategically placed here can be highly effective.

6. **Contrast**: Contrasting elements, whether through color, texture, or shape, create visual interest and draw attention. This can be particularly useful for highlighting key points.

Creating an Effective Visual Hierarchy

Crafting an effective visual hierarchy requires a deep understanding of the message you want to convey and the audience you want to reach. Here are some steps to help you create a strong visual hierarchy:

1. **Identify Key Messages**: Determine the most important messages or elements in your design. What do you want the viewer to notice first?

2. **Hierarchy Structure**: Create a hierarchical structure that organizes elements based on their

importance. This structure should guide the viewer's eye logically from the most important to the least important information.

3. **Use of Contrast**: Employ contrast strategically. Whether through size, color, or typography, use contrast to emphasize the most critical elements.

4. **Consistency**: Maintain consistency in your design. Use consistent fonts, colors, and styles for headings, subheadings, and body text to establish a clear visual order.

5. **Testing and Refinement**: Don't hesitate to test your design with actual users or colleagues. Their feedback can help identify areas where the hierarchy may need adjustment.

Visual Hierarchy in Practice

Visual hierarchy is ubiquitous in design, from web pages and posters to logos and infographics. Consider a website, for instance. The homepage typically features a large headline and a prominent call-to-action button, guiding users to explore further. On a product page, product images and prices are prioritized, with detailed descriptions and reviews placed lower on the page.

In conclusion, visual hierarchy is the secret sauce that transforms chaos into clarity in the world of design. By strategically arranging elements, you can lead your audience through the visual narrative, ensuring that your message is not only seen but also understood. As we delve deeper into the world of visual communication, you'll discover how to harness the power of visual hierarchy to create impactful designs.

Balance and Composition:

Creating Harmonious Visual Arrangements

In the world of visual communication, balance and composition are the dynamic duo that transforms a jumble of design elements into a harmonious and visually pleasing arrangement. Just as a well-orchestrated symphony combines different instruments to create a cohesive melody, balance and composition unite various visual elements to produce a unified and aesthetically pleasing whole.

The Essence of Balance

Balance in design refers to the distribution of visual elements to create equilibrium and stability in a composition. It's the art of ensuring that no single element dominates the design, resulting in an arrangement where everything feels just right. There are two primary types of balance:

1. **Symmetrical Balance**: In symmetrical designs, elements are evenly distributed on either side of a

central axis or a line of symmetry. This creates a sense of formal and classical order. Think of a perfectly symmetrical face or a balanced architectural facade.

2. **Asymmetrical Balance**: Asymmetrical designs achieve balance through the careful arrangement of dissimilar elements. Here, the visual weight is distributed unevenly but still results in equilibrium. Asymmetry is dynamic and often creates a sense of movement and interest. It's like a well-balanced seesaw with different weights on each end.

Composition: The Art of Arrangement

Composition, on the other hand, is the deliberate organization and arrangement of visual elements within a design. It's the process of deciding where each element will be placed, how they will interact, and what the overall structure of the design will be. Effective composition takes into account principles such as alignment, proximity, contrast, and whitespace.

Achieving Balance and Composition

Creating balance and composition requires a keen eye for aesthetics and a deep understanding of the message you want to convey. Here are key considerations for achieving these design principles:

1. **Symmetry or Asymmetry**: Choose the type of balance that suits your design's purpose. Symmetry can convey stability and formality, while asymmetry can add a touch of dynamism.

2. **Alignment**: Align elements consistently to create a sense of order. Elements that are misaligned can disrupt the visual flow.

3. **Proximity**: Group related elements together to show their relationship. For example, place a caption close to an image it describes.

4. **Contrast**: Use contrast in size, color, or shape to create visual interest and emphasize key elements.

5. **Whitespace**: Allow for ample whitespace (also known as negative space) to give your design breathing room and prevent clutter.

Balance and Composition in Practice

Balance and composition are fundamental in a wide range of design applications. In print and web design, a well-balanced layout ensures that text and images are legible and aesthetically pleasing. In photography, composition techniques such as the rule of thirds guide how subjects are framed. Even in the design of everyday objects like furniture or packaging, balance and composition play a vital role in functionality and aesthetics.

In conclusion, mastering balance and composition is akin to being a conductor, harmonizing disparate elements into a visual masterpiece. As we continue our journey through the principles of visual design, you'll discover how these techniques are applied in various contexts, from typography to color theory, enabling you to create designs that captivate and engage.

Typography in Visual Communication

The Art and Science of Text

Typography, the art and science of arranging type to make written language legible, readable, and visually appealing, is a cornerstone of visual communication. In this section, we'll explore the critical role that typography plays in design, from selecting the right typefaces to establishing hierarchy and enhancing the overall visual experience.

The Power of Typography

Typography is not just about choosing fonts; it's about conveying meaning through text. It's a silent yet eloquent storyteller that can evoke emotions, set the tone, and influence how information is perceived. Typography communicates a message before the words themselves are even read.

Font Choice Matters

The choice of typeface, or font, is one of the most crucial decisions a designer makes. Different fonts have distinct personalities and associations. For example:

- **Serif Fonts** (e.g., Times New Roman) convey tradition, formality, and reliability. They are often used in print publications and formal documents.

- **Sans-serif Fonts** (e.g., Helvetica) exude modernity, simplicity, and readability. They are commonly used in digital interfaces and contemporary design.

- **Script Fonts** (e.g., Brush Script) evoke elegance, creativity, and a personal touch. They are often seen in invitations and artistic designs.

- **Display Fonts** (e.g., Impact) are bold and attention-grabbing, suitable for headlines and signage.

Hierarchy through Typography

Typography is instrumental in establishing a visual hierarchy within a design. This hierarchy guides the viewer's eye and indicates the relative importance of different pieces of text. For instance:

- **Headings** are typically set in larger, bolder fonts to signal major sections or topics.

- **Subheadings** may be slightly smaller but still distinct to provide a clear structure.

- **Body Text** uses a legible font size and style for comfortable reading.

- **Emphasis** can be added through italics, bolding, or different font weights.

Spacing and Kerning

Beyond choosing the right typeface, spacing and kerning are vital aspects of typography. Adequate spacing between letters (kerning) and lines (leading) enhances readability and ensures that text flows smoothly. Poor spacing can make text difficult to read and disrupt the visual harmony of a design.

Alignment and Consistency

Consistency in typography is key to creating a polished and professional look. Ensure that fonts, font sizes, and alignment are consistent throughout your design. Misaligned text or inconsistent font choices can undermine the visual hierarchy and overall impact.

Legibility and Readability

While aesthetics are important, never compromise on legibility and readability. Ensure that your chosen typeface and font size are appropriate for the medium and audience. What looks elegant in a headline may not work for long paragraphs of text.

In conclusion, typography is both an art and a science, requiring a delicate balance between aesthetics and functionality. It's the designer's tool to infuse text with meaning, structure information, and enhance the overall visual experience. As we journey through the principles of visual design, typography will continue to be a thread that weaves through various design contexts, from print to digital media.

Color Psychology

Communicating Emotions Through Color

Colors are not just visual elements; they are potent conveyors of emotions and messages. In this section, we venture into the world of color psychology, where hues and shades become the language of feelings and meanings. Understanding how colors impact human perception is vital for creating designs that resonate with your audience.

The Emotional Language of Colors

Colors have the remarkable ability to evoke emotions, trigger memories, and influence behavior. This phenomenon, known as color psychology, explores the psychological and emotional impact of different colors. Here are some key emotions and associations commonly linked to colors:

- **Red**: Passion, excitement, love, but also danger or warning.

- **Blue**: Trust, calmness, stability, but also sadness or coldness.

- **Green**: Growth, nature, health, but also envy or inexperience.

- **Yellow**: Happiness, optimism, energy, but also caution or anxiety.

- **Purple**: Royalty, luxury, creativity, but also mystery or extravagance.

- **Orange**: Warmth, enthusiasm, creativity, but also aggression or caution.

- **Black**: Elegance, power, sophistication, but also mystery or darkness.

- **White**: Purity, simplicity, cleanliness, but also emptiness or coldness.

Color Harmony and Combinations

Effective use of color extends beyond individual color choices. Designers must consider color harmony and combinations to create visually pleasing compositions. Key principles in this regard include:

- **Complementary Colors**: Colors opposite each other on the color wheel, such as red and green or blue and orange, create strong contrast and visual interest.

- **Analogous Colors**: Colors adjacent to each other on the color wheel, like various shades of blue, green, and teal, create a harmonious and calming effect.

- **Monochromatic Color Schemes**: Using variations of a single color, such as different shades of blue, creates a clean and sophisticated look.

- **Triadic Color Schemes**: Selecting three equidistant colors on the color wheel, such as red, yellow, and blue, can result in a vibrant and balanced composition.

Cultural and Contextual Influences

It's important to note that the emotional associations of colors can vary across cultures and contexts. For example, while white symbolizes purity and weddings in Western cultures, it may signify mourning in some Eastern cultures. Context matters, and designers should be mindful of cultural sensitivities and preferences when selecting colors for international audiences.

The Role of Color in Branding

Color plays a significant role in branding and marketing. Brands often choose specific colors to convey their values, establish recognition, and create emotional connections with consumers. For example, the warm red of Coca-Cola elicits a sense of excitement, while the soothing blue of Facebook promotes trust and reliability.

Creating Emotional Impact

As a designer, understanding color psychology empowers you to create designs that elicit the desired emotional responses from your audience. Whether you're designing a website, a product package, or a marketing campaign, your color choices can make a profound difference in how your message is received and remembered.

In summary, color psychology is a fascinating exploration of how colors can communicate emotions and messages. As we continue our journey through the principles of visual design, keep in mind that the colors you choose have the power to engage, inspire, and leave a lasting impression.

Chapter 3: Common Mistakes in Visual Design

Cluttered Designs

Clutter can be the nemesis of effective visual communication. In this subchapter, we'll explore the common pitfall of cluttered designs and how they can hinder the conveyance of your message. We'll also discuss strategies for achieving clarity and visual harmony in your designs.

The Perils of Clutter

A cluttered design overwhelms the viewer with an excess of visual information. It's like trying to have a conversation in a noisy, crowded room— your message gets lost in the chaos. Clutter can take various forms, including:

- **Too Many Elements**: When a design is crowded with elements like text, images, and graphics, it becomes difficult for the viewer to focus on what's essential.

- **Chaotic Layout**: Disorganized placement of elements can confuse the viewer's eye, making it challenging to follow a logical flow.

- **Overuse of Color**: Excessive use of color, especially vibrant and contrasting hues, can create visual noise that distracts from the core message.

- **Lack of Whitespace**: Insufficient whitespace (negative space) makes a design feel cramped and overwhelming.

35

Achieving Clarity

To combat clutter and achieve clarity in your designs, consider the following strategies:

1. **Prioritize Information**: Determine the most critical elements or messages and ensure they take center stage. Less important details should take a backseat or be omitted.

2. **Simplify Layout**: Create a clean and organized layout with ample whitespace to guide the viewer's eye. Use grids and alignment to maintain structure.

3. **Consistent Typography**: Use a consistent and legible typeface for all text elements. Maintain a clear hierarchy with headings, subheadings, and body text.

4. **Selective Use of Color**: Employ color intentionally to draw attention to key elements or create visual harmony. Avoid an excess of conflicting colors.

5. **Less Is More**: Embrace minimalism. Remember that simplicity often leads to more effective communication. Sometimes, a single well-chosen image or a concise message can be more powerful than a cluttered composition.

6. **User Testing**: When possible, conduct user testing to gather feedback from your audience. This can

reveal areas of confusion or overwhelm in your design.

Examples of Cluttered Designs

To illustrate the impact of clutter, we'll explore real-world examples of cluttered designs and discuss how these designs could be improved for better clarity and communication.

1. Website Landing Page:

- **Cluttered Elements**: An overloaded landing page with multiple pop-ups, banners, social media feeds, and a plethora of links and buttons can overwhelm visitors.

- **Improvement**: Simplify the landing page by focusing on a clear call to action (CTA), removing excessive distractions, and organizing content in a clean, hierarchical manner.

2. Poster for an Event:

- **Cluttered Elements**: Event posters with too many fonts, colors, and graphics can make it difficult for viewers to grasp essential information quickly.

- **Improvement**: Streamline the design by using a consistent font, color scheme, and hierarchy to prioritize event details like date, time, and location.

3. Product Packaging:

- **Cluttered Elements**: Some product packaging features excessive text, images, and promotional stickers, making it challenging for consumers to identify the product's core features.

- **Improvement**: Focus on minimalist packaging that highlights the product's key benefits and uses clear, concise text and visuals to convey its value.

4. Email Newsletter:

- **Cluttered Elements**: Overloaded email newsletters with too many images, buttons, and links can confuse recipients and decrease click-through rates.

- **Improvement**: Simplify the email by having a single, clear message, reducing the number of images, and providing a well-structured layout that guides readers.

5. PowerPoint Presentation:

- **Cluttered Elements**: Slides with excessive bullet points, text, and complex graphics can overwhelm the audience and hinder information retention.

- **Improvement**: Create visually appealing slides with concise text, clear visuals, and a logical flow of information, allowing the audience to absorb key points easily.

6. Magazine Advertisement:

- **Cluttered Elements**: Magazine ads that cram too much information, such as multiple product images, slogans, and fine print, can detract from the main message.

- **Improvement**: Opt for a cleaner layout that highlights one or two key product features or benefits, using a captivating image and minimal text.

7. Retail Store Window Display:

- **Cluttered Elements**: Store displays with overcrowded merchandise can overwhelm shoppers and make it challenging to focus on individual products.

- **Improvement**: Create visually appealing displays that feature a curated selection of products, allowing each item to shine and making it easier for customers to browse.

In each of these examples, simplifying the design by removing unnecessary elements, prioritizing key information, and maintaining visual consistency can greatly improve clarity and communication. Cluttered designs can lead to confusion and frustration, while streamlined and well-organized designs enhance the user experience and convey messages more effectively.

Ineffective Use of Color

Color is a powerful tool in visual design, but its misuse can lead to confusion and miscommunication. In this subchapter, we delve into the common mistake of ineffective use of color and how it can impact the success of your designs. We'll also discuss strategies for harnessing color's potential effectively.

The Pitfalls of Ineffective Color Choices

Ineffective use of color can be detrimental to your design in several ways:

1. **Clashing Color Combinations**: Using colors that clash or create visual discomfort can repel viewers rather than engage them.

2. **Color Overload**: An overabundance of colors can overwhelm the viewer and dilute the impact of the design.

3. **Color Blindness Considerations**: Ignoring color blindness can lead to exclusion of individuals with color vision deficiencies from understanding your message.

4. **Inconsistent Color Usage**: Lack of consistency in color choices can create confusion and hinder the establishment of brand identity.

5. **Misalignment with Message**: Colors should align with the message or tone you wish to convey. Inconsistent color choices can mislead or confuse your audience.

Strategies for Effective Use of Color

To avoid the pitfalls of ineffective color use, consider the following strategies:

1. **Color Harmony**: Use color schemes that create harmony and convey the desired emotions. Explore complementary, analogous, or monochromatic color palettes.

2. **Contrast**: Ensure there is enough contrast between text and background colors to ensure readability. Use contrasting colors to emphasize important elements.

3. **Accessibility**: Design with accessibility in mind. Provide alternative text for images, use text that remains readable even without color, and check your designs with color blindness simulators.

4. **Consistency**: Establish a consistent color palette for your brand or project. This helps in brand recognition and maintaining a cohesive look and feel.

5. **Testing**: Test your color choices with a diverse audience, including individuals with color vision

deficiencies. Their feedback can help identify potential issues.

Real-World Examples

To illustrate the concept of ineffective use of color, we'll examine real-world examples of designs where color choices hinder the effectiveness of the message. By analyzing these examples, you'll gain insights into how color can impact perception and what to avoid in your own designs.

1. Restaurant Menu:

- **Issue**: A restaurant menu with a cluttered design that uses a wide range of vibrant colors for text and backgrounds, making it difficult to read and causing visual discomfort.

- **Improvement**: Use a limited color palette and ensure sufficient contrast between text and background for improved readability. Categorize menu items with subtle color accents, making it easier for customers to navigate.

2. Infographic for Health Tips:

- **Issue**: An infographic intended to convey health tips uses neon and clashing colors, creating a chaotic and distracting visual experience.

- **Improvement**: Opt for a harmonious color scheme that aligns with the topic. Use color to highlight key points and guide the viewer's eye through the information in a logical flow.

3. Website for Financial Services:

- **Issue**: A financial services website features a bright, contrasting color scheme with neon green buttons and red text, which can create a sense of urgency and anxiety for users seeking financial information.

- **Improvement**: Choose a calm and professional color palette that instills trust and reliability. Utilize green for positive actions like "Learn More" and reserve red for critical alerts.

4. Corporate Presentation Slides:

- **Issue**: A corporate presentation uses an inconsistent color scheme, with different fonts and background colors on each slide, leading to a disjointed and unprofessional look.

- **Improvement**: Establish a brand-appropriate color scheme and use it consistently across all slides. Maintain a clear hierarchy of colors for headings, text, and backgrounds.

5. Packaging for Children's Toys:

- **Issue**: Packaging for children's toys incorporates a mix of bright, clashing colors that can be visually overwhelming and confusing for both parents and children.

- **Improvement**: Adopt a more cohesive and child-friendly color palette that resonates with the target audience. Use colors strategically to guide attention to product features and benefits.

6. Poster for a Charity Event:

- **Issue**: A poster promoting a charity event uses muted and dull colors, which fail to capture attention and convey the urgency of the cause.

- **Improvement**: Select colors that align with the charity's mission and purpose, evoking emotions and motivating action. Brighter colors and contrasting elements can make the poster more impactful.

In these examples, ineffective use of color hinders the effectiveness of the message by causing visual discomfort, confusion, or a lack of alignment with the intended tone or audience. By analyzing these examples, designers can learn valuable lessons about the importance of color choices in conveying messages and ensuring positive user experiences.

Poor Font Choices

Typography is a critical aspect of design, and choosing the wrong fonts can lead to confusion and hinder the effectiveness of your visual communication. In this subchapter, we explore the common mistake of making poor font choices and how it impacts your design. We'll also discuss strategies for selecting the right fonts to enhance your message.

The Consequences of Poor Font Choices

Selecting inappropriate fonts for your design can have several negative consequences:

1. **Legibility Issues**: Fonts that are difficult to read can frustrate your audience and deter them from engaging with your content.

2. **Mismatched Tone**: Fonts carry personalities and tones. Choosing fonts that don't align with your message can send mixed signals.

3. **Lack of Consistency**: Inconsistent font choices disrupt the visual harmony of your design and can confuse your audience.

4. **Accessibility Concerns**: Some fonts may not be accessible to individuals with visual impairments. Ignoring accessibility can alienate a portion of your audience.

5. **Lost Brand Identity**: Poor font choices can weaken your brand identity, making it less memorable and recognizable.

Strategies for Effective Font Choices

To avoid the pitfalls of poor font choices, consider the following strategies:

1. **Legibility and Readability**: Prioritize legibility and readability above all else. Ensure that your chosen fonts are easy to read, especially in longer passages of text.

2. **Font Pairing**: Use font pairings that complement each other. Combining a serif font with a sans-serif font, for example, can create visual interest and establish hierarchy.

3. **Consider the Message**: Match your font choices to the tone and message of your design. Playful fonts may be suitable for a children's book but not for a legal document.

4. **Accessibility**: Choose fonts that are accessible and consider providing alternative formats or text for individuals with visual impairments.

5. **Consistency**: Establish a consistent set of fonts for your brand or project. This consistency helps in reinforcing brand identity and maintaining visual coherence.

Real-World Examples

To illustrate the concept of poor font choices, we'll analyze real-world examples of designs where font selection hinders the effectiveness of the message. These examples will provide insights into how font choices can impact perception and help you make informed decisions in your own designs.

1. Restaurant Menu:

- **Issue**: A restaurant menu uses a playful, decorative font for item descriptions, making it challenging for customers to quickly read and understand the dishes.

- **Improvement**: Select a legible, sans-serif font for menu descriptions to enhance readability while reserving decorative fonts for headings or logos.

2. Legal Document:

- **Issue**: A legal document utilizes a cursive or script font for the main body text, which can be difficult to read, especially for complex legal language.

- **Improvement**: Choose a professional and legible serif font, such as Times New Roman or Georgia, for legal documents to ensure clarity and readability.

3. Corporate Website:

- **Issue**: A corporate website uses a wide variety of fonts across different sections, creating a disjointed and unprofessional appearance.

- **Improvement**: Establish a consistent font family and style guide for the website, ensuring that fonts align with the brand's identity and maintain visual coherence.

4. Educational Material for Children:

- **Issue**: Educational materials for children use a font that lacks clarity, making it challenging for young readers to recognize and differentiate letters.

- **Improvement**: Select a child-friendly font that emphasizes legibility and readability, ensuring that it aids in the learning process.

5. Technology Startup Logo:

- **Issue**: A technology startup's logo incorporates a complex and intricate font that is challenging to decipher, diminishing the brand's recognition.

- **Improvement**: Simplify the logo's font to enhance clarity and memorability, ensuring that it is easily recognizable across various platforms.

6. Magazine Article Layout:

- **Issue**: A magazine article layout uses a font size and style that lacks readability, especially in low-light settings, discouraging readers from engaging with the content.

- **Improvement**: Opt for a legible and appropriately sized serif or sans-serif font for body text, taking into account various reading conditions.

In these examples, poor font choices hinder the effectiveness of the message by causing readability issues, inconsistency, or a lack of alignment with the intended tone or audience. By analyzing these examples, designers can gain a deeper understanding of how font choices impact perception and how to select fonts that enhance communication and user experience.

Lack of Consistency

Consistency is a cornerstone of effective visual communication. In this subchapter, we'll delve into the common mistake of lacking consistency in your designs and how it can diminish the impact of your message. We'll also discuss strategies for achieving and maintaining visual consistency in your projects.

The Pitfalls of Inconsistency

Inconsistency in design can lead to a range of issues:

1. **Confusion**: Viewers may struggle to understand your message if design elements change abruptly throughout a project.

2. **Loss of Brand Identity**: Inconsistent branding can weaken your brand's recognition and impact.

3. **Visual Discomfort**: Frequent changes in design elements, such as fonts or color palettes, can create visual discomfort.

4. **Unprofessional Appearance**: Inconsistent designs can appear unprofessional and diminish the credibility of your project or brand.

5. **User Experience**: Inconsistent user interfaces can confuse and frustrate users, leading to a poor user experience.

Strategies for Achieving Consistency

To avoid the pitfalls of inconsistency, consider the following strategies:

1. **Brand Guidelines**: Establish clear brand guidelines that include specifications for fonts, colors, logos, and other design elements. These guidelines serve as a reference for maintaining consistency.

2. **Design Systems**: Create design systems that outline how design elements should be used consistently across various media, from websites to marketing materials.

3. **Templates**: Use templates for recurring design projects. Templates help ensure that design elements are applied consistently.

4. **Version Control**: Implement version control systems for collaborative projects to prevent unauthorized changes that can introduce inconsistency.

5. **Regular Audits**: Periodically audit your designs to ensure they align with established guidelines and standards.

Real-World Examples

To illustrate the concept of lacking consistency, we'll examine real-world examples of designs that suffer from inconsistency and discuss how consistency could enhance their effectiveness. These examples will provide practical insights into the impact of design consistency on perception.

1. Corporate Branding Materials:

- **Issue**: A company's branding materials, such as business cards, brochures, and the website, feature inconsistent use of colors, fonts, and logo variations.

- **Impact**: Lack of consistency dilutes the brand identity and confuses customers about the company's message and values.

- **Improvement**: Establish brand guidelines that dictate the use of specific colors, fonts, and logo versions across all materials to ensure a cohesive and recognizable brand presence.

2. E-commerce Website:

- **Issue**: An online store's product pages have inconsistent product image sizes, layout styles, and navigation menus, creating a disjointed shopping experience.

- **Impact**: Lack of consistency disrupts the user's journey, making it challenging to browse and compare products effectively.

- **Improvement**: Implement a consistent layout structure, standardized image sizes, and navigation menus across all product pages to enhance the user's shopping experience.

3. Newsletter Campaign:

- **Issue**: A company's email newsletter campaign features varied email templates with different color schemes, fonts, and layouts for each edition.

- **Impact**: Inconsistency can confuse subscribers and reduce brand recognition, making it challenging to establish a cohesive message.

- **Improvement**: Design a standardized email template that incorporates the company's brand colors, fonts, and layout, maintaining consistency across all newsletter editions.

4. Social Media Profiles:

- **Issue**: A brand's social media profiles display inconsistent profile pictures, cover photos, and post styles, leading to a fragmented online presence.

- **Impact**: Lack of consistency can weaken the brand's identity and make it less memorable on social media platforms.

- **Improvement**: Maintain consistent profile and cover photo styles, use a unified color scheme, and establish a posting schedule that aligns with the brand's message and values.

5. Marketing Collateral for an Event:

- **Issue**: Marketing collateral for an event, such as flyers and posters, use different fonts, colors, and imagery across various promotional materials.

- **Impact**: Inconsistency can confuse potential attendees and diminish the event's professionalism and credibility.

- **Improvement**: Develop a comprehensive design theme and guidelines for all event materials, ensuring a consistent visual identity to attract and inform attendees effectively.

6. Product Packaging Redesign:

- **Issue**: A brand redesigns its product packaging, but some products feature the new design while others still carry the old design, creating confusion for consumers.

- **Impact**: Inconsistency in product packaging can erode brand trust and make it difficult for consumers to identify the brand's products.

- **Improvement**: Implement a phased transition to the new packaging design to ensure consistency across all product lines and minimize confusion among customers.

In these examples, a lack of consistency in design elements, such as colors, fonts, layouts, and branding materials, diminishes the effectiveness of the message and the overall user experience. By recognizing the importance of design consistency and applying it strategically, organizations can convey a unified message and strengthen their brand identity.

Ignoring Accessibility

Accessibility in design is not just a nicety; it's a fundamental aspect of ensuring that your content is inclusive and reaches the widest audience possible. In this subchapter, we'll delve into the common mistake of ignoring accessibility in your designs and how it can lead to exclusion and communication barriers. We'll also discuss strategies for making your designs more accessible to all.

The Consequences of Ignoring Accessibility

Ignoring accessibility considerations in design can have serious consequences:

1. **Exclusion**: Inaccessible designs can exclude individuals with disabilities, such as those with visual or hearing impairments, from accessing your content.

2. **Legal Implications**: In some regions, there are legal requirements to ensure digital content is accessible to all, and non-compliance can lead to legal issues.

3. **Poor User Experience**: Inaccessible designs can result in a frustrating and subpar user experience for those who struggle to access or understand the content.

4. **Missed Opportunities**: By excluding individuals with disabilities, you miss the opportunity to engage with a significant portion of your potential audience.

Strategies for Ensuring Accessibility

To avoid the pitfalls of ignoring accessibility, consider the following strategies:

1. **Alt Text for Images**: Provide descriptive alt text for images so that screen readers can convey the content to users with visual impairments.

2. **Semantic HTML**: Use semantic HTML elements to provide structure and meaning to your content. For example, use headings to create a clear hierarchy of information.

3. **Contrast and Color**: Ensure there is sufficient contrast between text and background colors to make content readable for individuals with low vision.

4. **Keyboard Accessibility**: Ensure that all interactive elements can be navigated and activated using a keyboard alone, as some users may not be able to use a mouse.

5. **Transcripts and Captions**: Include transcripts for audio content and captions for video content to make them accessible to individuals with hearing impairments.

6. **Responsive Design**: Create responsive designs that adapt to various screen sizes and devices, accommodating users with different needs.

Real-World Examples

To illustrate the concept of ignoring accessibility, we'll examine real-world examples of designs that do not prioritize accessibility and discuss how accessibility improvements could enhance these designs. These examples will provide practical insights into the impact of accessibility on inclusivity and usability.

1. Government Website:

- **Issue**: A government website lacks alt text for images, making it inaccessible to individuals with visual impairments who rely on screen readers.

- **Impact**: Ignoring accessibility excludes a significant portion of the population from accessing critical government information and services.

- **Improvement**: Implement comprehensive alt text descriptions for all images on the website to ensure accessibility for users with visual impairments.

2. Mobile Application:

Issue: A mobile app features small, non-adjustable fonts and lacks options for users to resize text, making it challenging for people with low vision to use.

- **Impact**: Neglecting text size customization excludes users with visual impairments and reduces the app's overall usability.

- **Improvement**: Enable text resizing options within the app settings and ensure that fonts are resizable, providing an inclusive experience for all users.

3. E-commerce Website Checkout Process:

- **Issue**: An e-commerce website's checkout process contains color-coded error messages without accompanying text descriptions, rendering it unusable for individuals with color blindness.

- **Impact**: Ignoring accessibility results in frustration for users with color vision deficiencies who cannot decipher error messages.

- **Improvement**: Supplement color-coding with text descriptions or symbols to convey error messages effectively, ensuring a seamless checkout experience for all users.

4. Social Media Platform:

- **Issue**: A social media platform lacks keyboard navigation support and relies heavily on mouse interactions, making it inaccessible to individuals who rely on keyboard-only navigation.

- **Impact**: Neglecting keyboard accessibility excludes users with motor disabilities from participating fully in the platform.

- **Improvement**: Implement robust keyboard navigation functionalities and ensure that all interactive elements can be accessed and used via keyboard input.

5. Video Streaming Service:

- **Issue**: A video streaming service fails to provide closed captions for its video content, excluding individuals who are deaf or hard of hearing.

- **Impact**: Ignoring accessibility prevents users with hearing impairments from enjoying the content and understanding the dialogue.

- **Improvement**: Integrate closed captioning options for all video content to ensure accessibility and inclusivity for all viewers.

6. Online Forms for Customer Support:

- **Issue**: Online customer support forms do not include labels or instructions, making it difficult for individuals with cognitive disabilities to understand and complete the forms.

- **Impact**: Neglecting accessibility makes it challenging for users with cognitive impairments to seek assistance or provide feedback.

- **Improvement**: Incorporate clear labels, instructions, and simple language into online forms to enhance usability and accessibility for all users.

In these examples, ignoring accessibility considerations results in exclusion and usability challenges for various user groups. By prioritizing accessibility improvements, organizations can create more inclusive and user-friendly designs that accommodate individuals with disabilities and enhance the overall user experience.

Common Mistakes

In the previous subchapters, we've discussed several common mistakes that designers can make in their visual communication efforts. Continuing our journey through this chapter, we'll uncover more pitfalls to avoid and strategies to ensure your designs are effective and impactful.

Lack of Clear Call to Action

A clear call to action (CTA) is essential for guiding your audience on the next steps to take. Ignoring or having an unclear CTA can lead to missed opportunities and a lack of engagement.

- **Consequences**: Without a clear CTA, viewers may not know what action to take, resulting in inaction or confusion.

- **Strategies**: Make your CTAs concise and action-oriented. Use contrasting colors or styling to make them stand out.

Neglecting Mobile-Friendly Design

In our increasingly mobile-centric world, neglecting mobile-friendly design can alienate a significant portion of your audience.

- **Consequences**: Inaccessible or poorly designed mobile experiences can frustrate users and lead to high bounce rates.

- **Strategies**: Implement responsive design principles to ensure your content adapts seamlessly to various screen sizes and devices.

Overlooking User Testing and Feedback

Failure to gather user feedback and conduct testing can result in designs that do not resonate with your target audience.

- **Consequences**: You risk creating designs that miss the mark or fail to address user needs and preferences.

- **Strategies**: Engage in usability testing, gather feedback from real users, and use this information to refine and improve your designs.

Failing to Tell a Story

Visual communication is not just about conveying information; it's about telling a story and connecting with your audience on an emotional level.

- **Consequences**: Failing to tell a compelling story can result in disengagement and a lack of impact.

- **Strategies**: Craft narratives that resonate with your audience, invoke emotions, and create memorable experiences through your designs.

Ignoring Trends and Evolution

Design trends and technologies are constantly evolving. Ignoring these changes can make your designs appear outdated and less relevant.

- **Consequences**: Outdated designs can convey a lack of innovation or relevance.

- **Strategies**: Stay up-to-date with design trends, emerging technologies, and evolving user expectations to keep your designs fresh and modern.

As we continue to explore these common mistakes and strategies for avoiding them, you'll gain a deeper understanding of the principles that underlie effective visual communication.

Chapter 4: Tips for Effective Visual Communication

Simplicity in Design

Simplicity in design is a guiding principle that emphasizes the importance of clarity and minimalism. It's about distilling your message to its essence and presenting it in a straightforward and easily understandable manner. In this subtopic, we'll explore the benefits of simplicity and strategies for achieving it in your designs.

The Power of Simplicity

Simplicity is not about oversimplification but rather about removing unnecessary complexity and distractions. Here's why simplicity in design is crucial:

1. **Clarity**: Simple designs communicate your message clearly and concisely, ensuring that viewers understand your intended message without confusion.

2. **Focus**: Simplicity allows you to highlight the most critical elements, ensuring that your audience's attention is directed to what matters most.

3. **Memorability**: Simple, elegant designs are often more memorable and leave a lasting impression.

4. **Versatility**: Simple designs are versatile and can be adapted to various contexts and platforms.

Strategies for Achieving Simplicity

To infuse simplicity into your designs, consider the following strategies:

1. **Prioritize Content**: Focus on your core message or content and eliminate anything that doesn't contribute to it.

2. **Whitespace**: Embrace whitespace (negative space) to provide breathing room and create a sense of balance in your design.

3. **Clear Hierarchy**: Establish a clear hierarchy of information using fonts, colors, and layout to guide the viewer's eye.

4. **Consistency**: Maintain consistency in design elements like fonts, colors, and spacing throughout your project.

5. **Remove Clutter**: Identify and remove any unnecessary elements or distractions that clutter your design.

6. **Test and Iterate**: Conduct user testing to gather feedback on your design's simplicity and make improvements based on user insights.

Real-World Examples

To illustrate the concept of simplicity in design, we'll examine real-world examples of designs that effectively embrace simplicity. These examples will provide practical insights into how simplicity enhances visual communication and user experience.

Choosing the Right Color Palette

Color is a fundamental element of visual communication, and selecting the right color palette can significantly impact how your message is received and understood. In this subtopic, we'll explore the importance of choosing the right color palette and strategies for doing so effectively.

The Role of Color Palette

Color palettes are more than just aesthetic choices; they convey emotions, set the tone, and enhance visual appeal. Here's why choosing the right color palette is crucial:

1. **Emotional Impact**: Colors evoke emotions and associations. The right colors can align your design with the intended emotions of your message.

2. **Consistency**: A well-chosen color palette ensures consistency across your design, reinforcing brand identity and creating visual coherence.

3. **Accessibility**: Consider the accessibility of your color choices, ensuring that they are readable and usable by all, including individuals with color vision deficiencies.

4. **Cultural Sensitivity**: Different cultures may interpret colors differently, so consider the cultural context of your audience.

Strategies for Choosing the Right Color Palette

To select an effective color palette for your design, consider the following strategies:

1. **Define Your Message**: Understand the message and emotions you want to convey through your design. Different colors have distinct associations; align them with your message.

2. **Color Harmonies**: Explore color harmonies like complementary, analogous, or monochromatic palettes to create visual harmony and contrast.

3. **Accessibility**: Ensure that your color choices meet accessibility standards. Test your designs with color blindness simulators to check for readability.

4. **Brand Identity**: If applicable, align your color palette with your brand's established colors for consistency and recognition.

5. **Test and Refine**: Experiment with different color combinations and gather feedback to determine which palette best conveys your message.

Real-World Examples

To illustrate the concept of choosing the right color palette, we'll examine real-world examples of designs that effectively use color to enhance their message. These examples will provide practical insights into how color can impact perception and engagement.

Typography Best Practices

Typography is the art and science of arranging type to make written language both readable and visually appealing. In this subtopic, we'll delve into typography best practices, emphasizing the critical role it plays in conveying your message effectively.

The Significance of Typography

Typography isn't just about selecting fonts; it's about creating a visual language that enhances your message. Here's why typography matters:

1. **Readability**: Well-chosen typefaces and font sizes ensure that your text is easy to read, preventing viewer frustration.

2. **Hierarchy**: Typography helps establish a hierarchy of information, guiding the viewer's eye to key points and structuring content.

3. **Personality**: Different typefaces convey distinct personalities and emotions. Your font choices should align with your message and brand.

4. **Consistency**: Consistency in typography maintains visual harmony throughout your design, reinforcing brand identity.

Typography Best Practices

To make the most of typography in your visual communication, consider the following best practices:

1. **Font Selection**: Choose fonts that align with your message and target audience. Select a combination of fonts for headings, subheadings, and body text for hierarchy.

2. **Font Readability**: Ensure that your chosen fonts are legible, especially in longer passages of text.

Consider factors like font size, line spacing (leading), and letter spacing (kerning).

3. **Hierarchy**: Use font weights (e.g., bold, italic) and sizes to establish a clear hierarchy of information. Headings should be more prominent than body text.

4. **Consistency**: Maintain consistency in font choices and styles throughout your design. Avoid using too many different fonts, as it can lead to visual clutter.

5. **Alignment**: Align your text consistently to create a clean and organized layout. Pay attention to left, right, or center alignment as appropriate.

6. **Whitespace**: Use whitespace effectively to separate and frame text, making it easier to read and understand.

7. **Accessibility**: Ensure that your typography is accessible by using high-contrast text and providing alternatives for images with text.

Real-World Examples

To illustrate typography best practices, we'll examine real-world examples of designs that effectively use typography to enhance their messages. These examples will provide practical insights into how typography impacts readability and engagement.

1. Book Cover Design:

- **Example**: The cover of a best-selling novel uses a well-chosen font that reflects the book's genre and mood. The title is in a bold, easily readable serif font, while the author's name is in a complementary sans-serif font.

- **Impact**: The typography enhances the book's appeal, giving potential readers a sense of the story's tone and genre, making it more likely for them to pick up the book.

2. Magazine Layout:

- **Example**: A lifestyle magazine article uses a clear and legible sans-serif font for the body text, with larger, bolded headings in a contrasting serif font.

- **Impact**: Typography establishes a clear hierarchy, making the article easy to skim while maintaining readability for those who want to delve deeper into the content.

3. Tech Startup Website:

- **Example**: The website of a tech startup employs a clean and modern sans-serif font for body text and navigational elements. Important headings use a bold version of the same font.

- **Impact**: Typography communicates the brand's tech-savvy and contemporary image while ensuring an intuitive and readable user experience.

4. Coffee Shop Menu:

- **Example**: A coffee shop menu features a cursive font for its logo and headers, with a readable serif font for the coffee descriptions and prices.

- **Impact**: The typography choices create an inviting and warm atmosphere, reflecting the coffee shop's brand and making it easy for customers to choose their preferred brew.

5. Nonprofit Organization Brochure:

- **Example**: A nonprofit's brochure uses a consistent serif font throughout, ensuring readability for donors and supporters. Emphasis is added with bold font and italics where necessary.

- **Impact**: Typography helps convey the organization's mission clearly and persuasively, encouraging support and engagement.

6. Event Poster:

- **Example**: An event poster for a music festival employs a bold, decorative font for the event name, while the date, time, and venue information use a simple sans-serif font for clarity.

- **Impact**: Typography helps capture the essence and excitement of the event, making it visually appealing while providing essential information.

In these examples, typography best practices are employed to enhance readability, create visual appeal, and convey the intended message effectively. Thoughtful font selection, hierarchy, and consistency in typography contribute to the success of these designs across various contexts and media.

Creating Engaging Visuals

Visual elements play a pivotal role in capturing your audience's attention and conveying your message effectively. In this subtopic, we'll explore strategies for creating engaging visuals that enhance the impact of your designs.

The Power of Visuals

Visuals, such as images, graphics, and illustrations, can make your message more compelling and memorable. Here's why creating engaging visuals is crucial:

1. **Attention-Grabbing**: Engaging visuals capture viewers' attention and encourage them to explore your content further.

2. **Comprehension**: Visuals can simplify complex information, making it easier for viewers to understand and retain.

3. **Emotional Connection**: Well-chosen visuals can evoke emotions and create a deeper connection with your audience.

4. **Visual Storytelling**: Visuals are powerful tools for storytelling, allowing you to convey narratives and concepts effectively.

Strategies for Creating Engaging Visuals

To create visuals that captivate your audience, consider the following strategies:

1. **Relevance**: Ensure that visuals are directly related to your message and enhance its meaning. Avoid using visuals that are merely decorative.

2. **Quality**: Use high-quality images and graphics to maintain a professional and polished appearance.

3. **Originality**: Whenever possible, use original visuals that align with your brand or project's unique identity.

4. **Consistency**: Maintain a consistent style and theme for your visuals to reinforce brand recognition.

5. **Balance**: Avoid overcrowding your design with too many visuals. Balance text and visuals to create a harmonious composition.

6. **Accessibility**: Provide alternative descriptions or text for non-text content, ensuring that individuals with disabilities can access the information.

7. **Storytelling**: Use visuals to tell a story or convey a narrative that complements your message.

Real-World Examples

To illustrate the concept of creating engaging visuals, we'll examine real-world examples of designs that effectively use visuals to enhance their messages. These examples will provide practical insights into how visuals can impact perception and engagement.

1. Travel Website Homepage:

- **Example**: A travel website's homepage features a stunning, high-resolution image of a tropical beach as its background. The image immediately captures visitors' attention and invites them to explore the site's vacation packages.

- **Impact**: The engaging visual immerses users in the destination's beauty, sparking their wanderlust and encouraging them to explore the site's offerings.

2. Food Blog Post:

- **Example**: A food blog post showcasing a new recipe includes a series of high-quality, close-up images of the finished dish at various angles. Each image highlights the delicious details of the meal.

- **Impact**: Engaging visuals make the recipe more enticing, helping readers imagine the taste and appearance of the dish, increasing the likelihood they'll try the recipe themselves.

3. Social Media Advertisement:

- **Example**: A social media ad for a fitness brand uses a short video clip showing individuals of all fitness levels using the product during their workouts. The video's dynamic visuals convey inclusivity and effectiveness.

- **Impact**: Engaging visuals in the video capture the audience's attention and effectively communicate the product's benefits and suitability for diverse users.

4. Art Gallery Poster:

- **Example**: A poster advertising an art gallery exhibition features a collage of select artwork pieces. The collage provides a glimpse of the variety and quality of art on display.

- **Impact**: Engaging visuals in the poster stimulate curiosity and encourage art enthusiasts to visit the gallery to view the full collection.

5. Technology Product Packaging:

- **Example**: The packaging for a new smartphone showcases the product's sleek design through carefully composed images from different angles. The images highlight the phone's features and aesthetics.

- **Impact**: Engaging visuals on the packaging appeal to potential buyers by showcasing the product's design and functionality, making it more likely for them to make a purchase.

6. Environmental Awareness Campaign:

- **Example**: An environmental organization's campaign poster uses a striking image of a polluted beach juxtaposed with a pristine beach. The visual contrast highlights the urgency of environmental conservation.

- **Impact**: Engaging visuals in the poster evoke an emotional response and encourage viewers to take action to protect the environment.

In these examples, creating engaging visuals plays a pivotal role in capturing attention, conveying messages effectively, and encouraging desired actions. Whether it's a travel website, a food blog, social media advertising, or art promotion, visuals are a powerful tool for engagement and communication.

Embracing Minimalism

Minimalism is a design philosophy that emphasizes simplicity, clarity, and the removal of unnecessary elements. In this subtopic, we'll explore the concept of embracing minimalism in your visual communication efforts and how it can lead to more impactful designs.

The Essence of Minimalism

Minimalism is about focusing on the essentials and eliminating the superfluous. Here's why embracing minimalism can enhance your visual communication:

1. **Clarity**: Minimalist designs are clear and uncluttered, ensuring that your message is the center of attention.

2. **Visual Appeal**: Simplicity in design often results in a visually pleasing and elegant aesthetic.

3. **Memorability**: Minimalist designs are memorable because they leave a lasting impression with their simplicity and focus.

4. **Versatility**: Minimalist designs are versatile and can adapt to various contexts and media.

Strategies for Embracing Minimalism

To incorporate minimalism into your visual communication, consider the following strategies:

1. **Simplify Content**: Start by distilling your message or content to its essential components. Remove anything that doesn't contribute to the core message.

2. **Whitespace**: Make effective use of whitespace to create a sense of balance and allow your content to breathe.

3. **Limited Color Palette**: Embrace a limited color palette to maintain visual simplicity and cohesion.

4. **Typography**: Use clean and legible fonts. Minimize the number of font styles to maintain consistency.

5. **Remove Unnecessary Elements**: Identify and remove any unnecessary graphics, images, or text that add clutter.

6. **Hierarchy**: Establish a clear hierarchy of information using font weights, sizes, and layout to guide the viewer's eye.

7. **User-Centered Design**: Consider the needs and preferences of your target audience to create designs that resonate with them.

Real-World Examples

To illustrate the concept of embracing minimalism, we'll examine real-world examples of designs that effectively apply minimalist principles to enhance their messages. These examples will provide practical insights into how minimalism can impact the clarity and visual appeal of your designs.

1. Product Packaging:

- **Example**: The packaging for a luxury skincare brand uses a clean, white background with a simple logo and minimal text. The focus is on the product itself, which is showcased through a single, elegant image.

- **Impact**: Embracing minimalism in packaging conveys a sense of sophistication and purity, making the product appear premium and desirable.

2. Website Landing Page:

- **Example**: A tech startup's landing page features a minimalist design with ample white space, a clear headline, and a single call to action (CTA) button. There are no distracting elements or clutter.

- **Impact**: Minimalist design on the landing page ensures that visitors can easily understand the message and take the desired action, increasing conversion rates.

3. Art Exhibition Poster:

- **Example**: A poster promoting an art exhibition uses a simple, monochromatic color scheme with a minimalistic typography layout. The poster showcases one key artwork as the focal point.

- **Impact**: Embracing minimalism in the poster draws attention to the featured artwork and creates an air of sophistication, inviting art enthusiasts to the exhibition.

4. Book Cover Design:

- **Example**: The cover of a thought-provoking non-fiction book employs a minimalist approach with a single, impactful image or illustration and a subtle title and author's name.

- **Impact**: Minimalism in book cover design makes the book appear intriguing and thoughtfully designed, prompting potential readers to explore its contents.

5. Restaurant Menu:

- **Example**: A restaurant's menu adopts a minimalist design with a limited color palette, clean typography, and a straightforward layout that focuses on the dishes and their descriptions.

- **Impact**: Embracing minimalism in the menu design enhances readability, making it easier for diners to choose their meals and creating an impression of simplicity and quality.

6. Event Invitation:

- **Example**: An invitation to a corporate event features a minimalist design with a single, elegant typeface, and a subtle logo. There are no unnecessary decorations or embellishments.

- **Impact**: Minimalist design in the invitation conveys professionalism and sophistication, encouraging attendees to view the event as a valuable opportunity.

In these examples, embracing minimalism in design enhances clarity, visual appeal, and the overall effectiveness of the message. Whether it's packaging, web design, art promotion, book covers, menus, or event invitations, minimalism can create a sense of elegance, simplicity, and focus that resonates with audiences.

Chapter 5: Visual Communication in Advertising

Visual Storytelling

Visual storytelling is a powerful technique in advertising that uses compelling visuals to convey a narrative, engage audiences, and leave a lasting impression. In this subtopic, we'll explore the art of visual storytelling in advertising and its impact on conveying messages effectively.

The Power of Visual Storytelling in Advertising

Visual storytelling is not just about showcasing products; it's about creating narratives that resonate with audiences. Here's why it's vital in advertising:

1. **Engagement**: Stories captivate and engage viewers, holding their attention longer than traditional ads.

2. **Emotional Connection**: Stories evoke emotions, making it easier for viewers to connect with and remember your brand or product.

3. **Brand Identity**: Effective visual storytelling helps define and reinforce your brand's identity.

4. **Memorability**: Well-crafted stories are memorable, leaving a lasting impression on viewers.

Strategies for Visual Storytelling in Advertising

To incorporate visual storytelling into your advertising efforts, consider the following strategies:

1. **Define Your Message**: Identify the core message or story you want to convey through your ad campaign.

2. **Character Development**: Create relatable characters or personas that audiences can connect with.

3. **Plot and Conflict**: Craft a compelling narrative with a clear plot and conflict, building tension and engagement.

4. **Visual Consistency**: Maintain visual consistency in your storytelling, using color palettes and design elements that align with your brand.

5. **Call to Action**: Ensure your story leads to a clear call to action (CTA) that encourages viewers to take the desired steps.

6. **Testing and Iteration**: Gather feedback and test different story elements to refine your storytelling approach.

Real-World Examples

To illustrate the concept of visual storytelling in advertising, we'll examine real-world examples of ad campaigns that effectively use storytelling techniques to engage and connect with their target audiences. These examples will provide practical insights into the power of storytelling in advertising.

1. Apple's "1984" Commercial:

- **Story**: This iconic Super Bowl commercial from Apple in 1984 told the story of rebellion against conformity. It portrayed a dystopian world where people were brainwashed, and a young woman representing the Macintosh computer shattered the conformity with a sledgehammer.

- **Impact**: The ad conveyed the message that Apple's Macintosh was a revolutionary product that challenged the status quo, and it generated immense buzz and anticipation.

2. Coca-Cola's "Holidays Are Coming" Campaign:

- **Story**: Coca-Cola's holiday ads often feature the iconic Coca-Cola truck traveling through snowy landscapes. It's a simple but effective story of joy, togetherness, and the holiday spirit.

- **Impact**: The ad became synonymous with the holiday season and Coca-Cola, creating a strong emotional connection with viewers and reinforcing the brand's association with festive celebrations.

3. Nike's "Dream Crazy" Campaign:

- **Story**: Nike's "Dream Crazy" campaign featured Colin Kaepernick, the former NFL quarterback known for his activism. The ad tells the story of athletes who have defied odds and societal expectations to achieve greatness.

- **Impact**: This campaign sparked conversations about social justice and became a symbol of Nike's support for athletes using their platform for positive change.

4. Google's "Dear Sophie" Ad:

- **Story**: Google's "Dear Sophie" ad tells the story of a father using Google products to document his daughter's life from birth to her first day of school. It's a heartwarming story of love and technology's role in preserving memories.

- **Impact**: The ad tugged at viewers' heartstrings, highlighting Google's products as tools for capturing and sharing meaningful moments.

5. Dove's "Real Beauty" Campaign:

- **Story**: Dove's "Real Beauty" campaign focuses on challenging traditional beauty standards. It tells the stories of real women and their journeys to self-acceptance.

- **Impact**: The campaign sparked conversations about body image and self-esteem, positioning Dove as a brand that supports authenticity and self-confidence.

6. Budweiser's "Puppy Love" Commercial:

- **Story**: This Super Bowl ad features a friendship between a puppy and a Clydesdale horse. The story centers on the bond between the two and their determination to stay together.

- **Impact**: The heartwarming story resonated with viewers, making it one of the most beloved Super Bowl commercials, reinforcing Budweiser's emotional connection with its audience.

These real-world examples showcase the power of visual storytelling in advertising. Each campaign crafted a compelling narrative that engaged viewers emotionally and helped create a strong brand identity. Visual storytelling goes beyond promoting products; it connects with audiences on a deeper level, leaving a lasting impact.

Creating Memorable Ad Campaigns

In the world of advertising, the ultimate goal is to capture the attention of the target audience, leave a lasting impression, and drive action. Creating memorable ad campaigns is an art and a science that combines creativity, storytelling, psychology, and strategic thinking. In this chapter, we'll delve into the strategies, techniques, and real-world examples that have shaped some of the most unforgettable advertising campaigns in history.

The Power of Memorable Ads

Memorable advertisements are not just about getting noticed; they're about establishing a deep connection with consumers. Such ads resonate emotionally, make people think, and often become part of popular culture. They can evoke laughter, tears, nostalgia, or a sense of awe. These emotional connections have the potential to turn casual consumers into loyal customers and brand advocates.

Understanding the Elements of Memorable Ads

Creating a memorable ad campaign involves several key elements:

1. **Compelling Storytelling:** Memorable ads often tell a story. Whether it's a narrative about overcoming obstacles, a heartwarming tale of human connection, or a humorous skit, storytelling engages viewers and makes the ad more relatable.

2. **Emotional Appeal:** Emotional advertising is highly effective because it taps into human feelings. Ads that evoke joy, sadness, anger, or surprise tend to be more memorable. Emotional

resonance creates a lasting imprint in the viewer's mind.

3. **Unique Visuals:** Visually striking ads are hard to forget. This could be due to impressive cinematography, memorable characters, or innovative graphics. Visuals play a crucial role in capturing attention.

4. **Catchy Slogans and Jingles:** A well-crafted slogan or jingle can embed itself in people's minds. Think of "Just Do It" from Nike or the classic McDonald's jingle, "I'm Lovin' It." These taglines become synonymous with the brands they represent.

5. **Surprise and Creativity:** Memorable ads often surprise viewers. They break conventions, challenge expectations, or introduce unexpected twists. Creativity that defies norms tends to stand out.

6. **Relatability and Relevance:** Ads that connect with viewers on a personal level tend to be more memorable. They address common problems or desires and offer solutions or aspirations.

Real-World Examples of Memorable Ad Campaigns

Now, let's explore real-world examples of memorable ad campaigns that have left an indelible mark:

1. **Coca-Cola's "Share a Coke" Campaign:** Coca-Cola's personalized approach, where bottles featured people's names, created a sense of personal connection. It encouraged consumers to share a Coke with friends and family, fostering a sense of unity and happiness.

2. **Apple's "1984" Super Bowl Commercial:** Directed by Ridley Scott, this iconic ad portrayed a dystopian future, broken by a young woman with a sledgehammer. It introduced the Macintosh computer as a revolutionary device challenging the status quo.

3. **Dove's "Real Beauty" Campaign:** Dove's campaign celebrated the diversity of women's bodies, challenging traditional beauty standards. It used real women as models and aimed to boost women's self-esteem by promoting a broader definition of beauty.

4. **Old Spice's "The Man Your Man Could Smell Like":** This humorous ad featured a suave, shirtless spokesman delivering rapid-fire comedy while demonstrating the benefits of Old Spice body wash. It became a viral sensation and revitalized the brand's image.

5. **Nike's "Dream Crazy" Campaign:** Featuring Colin Kaepernick, this campaign celebrated athletes who defied societal expectations. It ignited conversations about social justice and the role of athletes in advocating for change.

6. **Budweiser's Clydesdale Commercials:** Budweiser's heartwarming ads often feature Clydesdale horses. They evoke nostalgia and emotions, creating a strong brand identity associated with tradition and celebration.

The Science Behind Memorability

Beyond creativity and emotional impact, there's a science to creating memorable ads. Cognitive psychology plays a crucial role in understanding how our brains process and retain information from advertisements. Elements like repetition, simplicity, and the use of familiar visual cues can enhance memorability.

Repetition: Repeating a brand name, slogan, or visual element throughout an ad campaign helps reinforce memory. Consistency builds recognition and recall.

Simplicity: Keeping the message clear and straightforward aids memorability. Complex or cluttered ads can overwhelm viewers and make it harder for them to remember key details.

Familiarity: Utilizing familiar visual cues or symbols can tap into existing knowledge in the viewer's mind. When viewers recognize something, it's more likely to be remembered.

Neuroscience and Advertising: Advances in neuroscience have allowed advertisers to gain insights into how the brain responds to advertising stimuli. Neuroimaging studies show that emotionally charged ads activate the brain's reward centers, making them more likely to be remembered.

Conclusion

Creating memorable ad campaigns is both an art and a science. It involves crafting compelling stories, evoking emotions, and using psychology to capture and retain the audience's attention. The real-world examples we've explored demonstrate that memorable ads can leave a profound impact, shaping brand perception and consumer behavior. As you navigate the world of visual communication in advertising, remember that the most unforgettable campaigns often combine creativity, emotion, and scientific principles to make a lasting impression.

Case Studies in Advertising

In the realm of advertising, case studies serve as invaluable tools for analyzing and understanding the strategies, challenges, and successes behind memorable campaigns. By dissecting real-world examples, advertisers and marketers can extract valuable insights, learn from both triumphs and failures, and apply these lessons to future endeavors. In this section, we will delve into several captivating case studies that illuminate the intricacies of effective advertising.

1. Apple's "Get a Mac" Campaign

Apple's "Get a Mac" campaign, which ran from 2006 to 2009, remains a paragon of successful advertising. The campaign featured a personified Mac (played by actor Justin Long) and a personified PC (played by John Hodgman) engaging in humorous conversations that highlighted the Mac's superiority.

Objective: Apple aimed to differentiate itself from its PC competitors, emphasizing its user-friendly interface, reliability, and stylish design.

Key Strategies:

- **Simplicity**: The campaign maintained a simple, consistent format in each ad, making it easy for viewers to follow.

- **Personification**: By giving human attributes to computers, the campaign made the message relatable and engaging.

- **Humor**: The use of humor made the ads entertaining while effectively conveying product benefits.

Results: The campaign received critical acclaim and resonated with audiences. Apple's market share grew, and the Mac became synonymous with user-friendly computing.

2. Dove's "Real Beauty" Campaign

Dove's "Real Beauty" campaign, launched in the early 2000s, challenged conventional beauty standards by featuring real women of various shapes, sizes, and ethnicities in its advertisements.

Objective: Dove aimed to redefine beauty and boost women's self-esteem by promoting a more inclusive definition of attractiveness.

Key Strategies:

- **Realism**: The campaign showcased real women instead of models, fostering relatability.

- **Empowerment**: By celebrating diverse beauty, Dove encouraged women to embrace their uniqueness.

- **Psychological Appeal**: The campaign tapped into consumers' emotions by addressing issues of self-esteem and body image.

Results: Dove's campaign received widespread praise for its empowering message and authenticity, contributing to increased brand loyalty and sales.

3. Nike's "Just Do It" Campaign

Nike's iconic "Just Do It" campaign, launched in 1988, has become a cornerstone of the brand's identity. It features athletes of various backgrounds and abilities conquering challenges.

Objective: Nike aimed to inspire and motivate people to pursue their athletic ambitions, regardless of skill level.

Key Strategies:

- **Empowerment**: The campaign's tagline, "Just Do It," encourages action and perseverance.

- **Diversity**: Featuring athletes from diverse backgrounds resonates with a wide audience.

- **Emotion**: The ads often evoke strong emotions, reinforcing the brand's connection with consumers.

Results: "Just Do It" became one of the most recognizable slogans in the world, contributing significantly to Nike's enduring success.

4. Old Spice's "The Man Your Man Could Smell Like" Campaign

Old Spice's humorous "The Man Your Man Could Smell Like" campaign, launched in 2010, revitalized the brand's image by creating a viral sensation.

Objective: Old Spice sought to reposition itself as a modern and appealing brand for a younger audience.

Key Strategies:

- **Humor**: The ads were hilariously absurd and memorable, making them widely shareable.

- **Engagement**: Old Spice responded to viewer comments with personalized videos, creating an interactive experience.

- **Speed**: The campaign produced and released videos quickly to stay relevant.

Results: The campaign generated massive online engagement, increasing sales and making Old Spice a cultural phenomenon.

5. Airbnb's "Belong Anywhere" Campaign

Airbnb's "Belong Anywhere" campaign, which started in 2014, focused on the idea of connecting travelers with unique, local experiences through home-sharing.

Objective: Airbnb aimed to convey its mission of creating a sense of belonging for travelers worldwide.

Key Strategies:

- **Storytelling**: The campaign featured heartwarming stories of travelers and hosts forming genuine connections.

- **Inclusivity**: Airbnb showcased a diverse range of hosts and guests from around the world.

- **Community Building**: The campaign highlighted the sense of community and shared experiences.

Results: "Belong Anywhere" successfully communicated Airbnb's message, contributing to the company's rapid growth and global recognition.

These case studies illuminate the diverse strategies and approaches used by advertisers to create impactful campaigns. Whether through humor, emotion, inclusivity, or empowerment, effective advertising campaigns can resonate deeply with audiences, leaving a lasting impression that transcends traditional marketing boundaries. By studying these case studies, advertisers can gain valuable insights into the ever-evolving landscape of advertising and discover new ways to connect with consumers in a meaningful way.

Chapter 6: Visual Communication in Web Design

User-Centered Design

User-centered design (UCD) is a foundational principle in web design, focusing on creating websites that prioritize the needs, preferences, and behaviors of users. It involves a deep understanding of the target audience and crafting web experiences that are intuitive, enjoyable, and effective.

Key Principles of User-Centered Design:

1. **User Research:** UCD starts with comprehensive user research. Designers gather data on user demographics, behaviors, goals, and pain points through methods like surveys, interviews, and usability testing.

2. **User Personas:** Creating user personas helps designers empathize with and understand their audience better. Personas are fictional representations of typical users, including their characteristics, motivations, and goals.

3. **Usability Testing:** Regular usability testing involves real users navigating the website to identify issues, confusion points, and areas for improvement. This feedback informs iterative design changes.

4. **Information Architecture:** Organizing content and navigation in a way that aligns with users' mental models and makes it easy for them to find what they're looking for.

5. **User-Centered Prototyping:** Designers create prototypes and wireframes with user feedback in mind. This iterative process ensures that the final design is user-friendly.

6. **Accessibility:** UCD considers the accessibility needs of all users, including those with disabilities, by adhering to web accessibility guidelines (WCAG).

The Benefits of User-Centered Design:

- **Enhanced User Satisfaction:** Websites that prioritize user needs tend to be more user-friendly, resulting in higher user satisfaction and loyalty.

- **Reduced Bounce Rates:** UCD helps in keeping users engaged and reducing bounce rates, as visitors find what they need quickly.

- **Improved Conversion Rates:** User-centered design can lead to higher conversion rates, whether it's signing up for a newsletter, making a purchase, or taking another desired action.

- **Effective Communication:** By aligning the design with user expectations, websites can convey information and messages more effectively.

In an era where web users expect seamless and intuitive experiences, user-centered design is a critical component of successful web design. It ensures that the visual communication on a website is not just visually appealing but also highly functional and user-friendly.

Responsive Design

In the ever-evolving landscape of web design, ensuring that websites look and function well on various devices and screen sizes is paramount. Responsive design is the approach that addresses this challenge. It involves creating web experiences that adapt and respond to the user's device, whether it's a desktop computer, tablet, smartphone, or any other screen size in between.

Key Principles and Techniques of Responsive Design:

1. **Flexible Grid Layouts:** Responsive design uses flexible grid systems that adjust content and elements based on the screen width. This allows for a seamless transition from large desktop screens to smaller mobile screens.

2. **Media Queries:** CSS media queries are used to apply specific styles and layouts based on the device's screen size, resolution, and orientation. This ensures that content displays optimally.

3. **Fluid Images:** Images are designed to scale proportionally with the screen size, preventing them from overflowing or appearing too small on different devices.

4. **Mobile-First Approach:** Some designers start with the mobile version of a website and progressively enhance it for larger screens. This approach ensures a strong focus on the mobile user experience.

5. **Content Prioritization:** In responsive design, content prioritization is crucial. Designers decide what elements are most important and ensure they remain accessible and prominent on all devices.

6. **Testing and Debugging:** Extensive testing across various devices and browsers is essential to identify and fix issues related to responsiveness.

The Benefits of Responsive Design:

- **Improved User Experience:** Responsive websites adapt seamlessly to the user's device, ensuring that content is easily readable and navigable.

- **Broader Audience Reach:** With the proliferation of mobile devices, responsive design is essential for reaching a wide audience.

- **Search Engine Optimization (SEO):** Google and other search engines prioritize mobile-friendly websites in search results, making responsive design a crucial factor for SEO.

- **Maintenance Efficiency:** Maintaining a single responsive website is more efficient than managing multiple versions for different devices.

Responsive design not only enhances the visual communication of a website but also plays a pivotal role in ensuring that the user experience remains consistent and enjoyable across diverse devices. In an era where mobile usage continues to rise, responsive design is a fundamental aspect of modern web development.

Navigation and User Experience

Navigation and user experience (UX) are at the core of effective web design. They determine how users interact with a website, find information, and engage with its content. Navigational elements and the overall UX heavily influence how visitors perceive and engage with a site.

Key Considerations for Navigation and User Experience:

1. **Intuitive Navigation Menus:** Websites should have clear and intuitive navigation menus that help users quickly find what they're looking for.

Dropdown menus, mega-menus, or simple navigation bars are commonly used for this purpose.

2. **User-Centric Information Architecture:** The way content is organized and categorized (information architecture) should align with how users think and search for information. This involves creating a logical hierarchy of pages and content.

3. **Search Functionality:** For larger websites, an effective search function is essential. Users should be able to find specific content by entering keywords or phrases.

4. **Mobile-Friendly Navigation:** Mobile devices have different navigation needs. Designers should ensure that mobile navigation is easy to use with gestures, buttons, or icons.

5. **Consistency:** Consistency in navigation elements, such as menu placement and terminology, across all pages of a website contributes to a smoother user experience.

6. **User Flow Analysis:** Understanding how users move through a website (user flow) helps in optimizing navigation. Heatmaps and user flow analysis tools can provide insights into user behavior.

7. **Accessibility:** Websites should be designed with accessibility in mind, ensuring that all users,

including those with disabilities, can navigate and access content effectively.

Creating a Positive User Experience:

1. **Page Loading Speed:** Slow-loading pages can frustrate users. Optimizing page speed is critical for a positive UX.

2. **Mobile Responsiveness:** As mentioned earlier, ensuring that the site is responsive and mobile-friendly is crucial for an excellent UX.

3. **Clutter-Free Design:** Avoiding clutter and maintaining a clean, organized layout helps users focus on the content.

4. **Engaging Content:** Content should be engaging, informative, and easy to read. The use of headings, bullet points, and multimedia can enhance content presentation.

5. **Feedback and Validation:** Provide clear feedback when users interact with elements like forms or buttons. Ensure that forms are validated in real-time to prevent errors.

6. **A/B Testing:** A/B testing allows designers to compare different versions of a webpage to determine which one provides a better user experience.

7. **User Surveys and Feedback:** Collecting user feedback through surveys or feedback forms can uncover areas for improvement.

8. **Error Handling:** Design error messages that guide users on how to rectify errors, making the experience less frustrating.

The Impact on Visual Communication:

Navigation and UX design directly influence how visual elements are presented and interacted with on a website. An intuitive navigation system ensures that users can access visual content easily and understand the site's visual language. The user experience should complement the visual communication, providing a seamless and enjoyable journey through the website's visuals and content.

Case Studies in Web Design

Web design is a dynamic field, continuously evolving to meet the changing needs of users and technological advancements. Case studies provide invaluable insights into the strategies and methodologies used by designers to create exceptional web experiences. In this section, we will explore some compelling case studies that showcase the art and science of web design.

1. Airbnb: Redefining Travel Experiences

Objective: Airbnb aimed to revolutionize the way people travel by connecting travelers with unique, local accommodations.

Key Strategies:

- **User-Centric Design:** Airbnb's website prioritizes user needs, offering easy-to-use search and booking features.

- **Visual Storytelling:** High-quality images and detailed descriptions of accommodations convey the essence of each listing.

- **Community Building:** The inclusion of user reviews and host profiles fosters trust and a sense of belonging.

Results: Airbnb's user-focused design and storytelling approach transformed the travel industry, making it a go-to platform for travelers seeking authentic experiences.

2. Slack: Streamlining Team Communication

Objective: Slack sought to simplify team communication and collaboration in a digital workspace.

Key Strategies:

- **Clean and Intuitive Interface:** Slack's user interface is uncluttered, with clear navigation and a focus on conversation threads.

- **Seamless Integration:** Slack integrates with numerous third-party apps and services, enhancing productivity.

- **Customization:** Users can customize their Slack workspace with themes and integrations.

Results: Slack's user-friendly design and versatility made it a staple for businesses and teams worldwide, streamlining communication and boosting productivity.

3. Dropbox: Enhancing File Sharing and Storage

Objective: Dropbox aimed to provide a user-friendly solution for file storage and sharing across devices.

Key Strategies:

- **Simplicity:** Dropbox's design is straightforward, with a focus on drag-and-drop functionality.

- **Cross-Platform Compatibility:** Dropbox seamlessly syncs files across devices and platforms.

- **File Versioning:** Users can access previous versions of files, enhancing collaboration.

Results: Dropbox's user-centric design and seamless functionality established it as a leader in cloud storage and file sharing.

4. Medium: Empowering Content Creators

Objective: Medium sought to provide a platform for writers and content creators to share their stories.

Key Strategies:

- **Minimalist Design:** Medium's design is clean and unobtrusive, allowing content to take center stage.

- **Engagement Features:** Readers can highlight and comment on articles, fostering discussion.

- **Curated Content:** Medium curates content based on user interests, enhancing discoverability.

Results: Medium's focus on content and community engagement has made it a thriving platform for writers and readers alike.

5. Stripe: Simplifying Online Payments

Objective: Stripe aimed to simplify online payment processing for businesses of all sizes.

Key Strategies:

- **Developer-Focused Design:** Stripe's APIs and documentation cater to developers, making integration straightforward.

- **Transparent Pricing:** Pricing information is clear and accessible, promoting trust.

- **Security:** Stripe prioritizes security and compliance, essential for financial transactions.

Results: Stripe's developer-friendly design and commitment to security have made it a preferred choice for online businesses handling payments.

These case studies illustrate the importance of user-centric design, simplicity, functionality, and innovation in web design. By understanding and applying the principles and strategies exemplified in these cases, designers can create websites and digital experiences that resonate with users, meet their needs, and leave a lasting impression.

Chapter 7: Visual Communication in Branding

Building a Strong Visual Identity

In the competitive landscape of modern business, establishing a strong visual identity is paramount. Your visual identity encompasses all the visual elements that represent your brand, creating a cohesive and memorable image in the minds of consumers. It goes beyond just a logo; it includes colors, typography, imagery, and even the tone of your brand's communication.

Key Elements of Building a Strong Visual Identity:

1. **Logo Design:** Your logo is the cornerstone of your visual identity. It should be unique, easily recognizable, and reflect your brand's personality and values.

2. **Color Palette:** Choose a distinctive color palette that resonates with your brand's message. Colors evoke emotions and can convey different meanings, so select them carefully.

3. **Typography:** Consistent typography enhances brand recognition. Choose fonts that align with your brand's personality and ensure they are used consistently across all materials.

4. **Imagery and Graphics:** The choice of images and graphics can convey a lot about your brand.

Whether it's photography, illustrations, or icons, ensure they align with your brand's message.

5. **Visual Consistency:** Consistency is key to a strong visual identity. All visual elements should work together harmoniously and be used consistently across all touchpoints, from your website to your marketing materials.

6. **Storytelling:** Visual identity should tell a story about your brand. Use visuals to communicate your brand's values, history, and mission.

7. **Flexibility:** While consistency is vital, your visual identity should also be flexible enough to adapt to various mediums and formats while maintaining its core essence.

The Importance of a Strong Visual Identity:

- **Brand Recognition:** A strong visual identity makes your brand instantly recognizable, even in a crowded marketplace.

- **Trust and Credibility:** A well-crafted visual identity can convey trust and credibility, making consumers more likely to choose your brand.

- **Memorability:** Visual elements that stand out are more likely to be remembered, keeping your brand top of mind.

- **Differentiation:** A unique visual identity sets you apart from competitors and helps you carve out a distinct niche.

- **Consistency:** Visual consistency builds trust with consumers, reinforcing your brand's promises and values.

Building a strong visual identity is an ongoing process that requires attention to detail and a deep understanding of your brand's identity and values. It's an investment that pays off in brand recognition, trust, and long-term success.

Logo Design Principles

Logos are the visual keystone of a brand's identity. They serve as the face of a company or organization, instantly recognizable and carrying the weight of brand reputation. Effective logo design is a nuanced art, rooted in fundamental principles that ensure a logo's ability to communicate, resonate, and endure.

Key Principles of Logo Design:

1. **Simplicity:** A great logo is simple and uncluttered. It should convey the essence of the brand with clean lines and uncomplicated shapes. A complex

logo can be visually confusing and challenging to reproduce in various sizes and media.

2. **Memorability:** A memorable logo is one that sticks in the minds of viewers. It should be distinctive and unique, making it easy for people to recall and recognize. Simplicity often aids memorability.

3. **Relevance:** A logo must be relevant to the brand it represents. It should communicate the brand's identity, values, and offerings. A well-designed logo aligns with the brand's mission and resonates with its target audience.

4. **Versatility:** Logos must work well in various contexts and sizes. They should be scalable without losing clarity or impact. A versatile logo remains effective on business cards, billboards, websites, and more.

5. **Timelessness:** A logo should have lasting appeal. While trends come and go, a timeless logo transcends fashion, ensuring that it remains relevant and effective for years to come.

6. **Appropriateness:** The design elements within a logo should be appropriate for the industry and audience. For example, a logo for a children's toy brand will differ significantly from one for a law firm.

7. **Balance:** Achieving a harmonious balance of elements, such as text and imagery, is crucial. A

well-balanced logo is visually pleasing and easy to digest.

8. **Color Harmony:** Colors play a significant role in logo design. They should harmonize with the brand's identity and evoke appropriate emotions. Consider the psychology of colors when selecting a palette.

9. **Uniqueness:** A logo should be one of a kind. It should avoid similarities with other logos to prevent confusion and maintain distinctiveness.

The Design Process:

1. **Research:** Begin with research to understand the brand, its competitors, target audience, and industry trends. This knowledge informs the design process.

2. **Conceptualization:** Brainstorm and sketch ideas, exploring various concepts and directions. This phase often involves rough drafts and experimentation.

3. **Simplification:** Refine the concepts, focusing on simplifying the design. Eliminate unnecessary elements while retaining the core message.

4. **Digital Rendering:** Create digital versions of the chosen concept(s) using vector design software for precision and scalability.

5. **Feedback:** Gather feedback from stakeholders and peers to identify areas for improvement. Iterate on the design based on this input.

6. **Testing:** Test the logo in different contexts, sizes, and color variations to ensure it remains effective and versatile.

7. **Finalization:** Once the design meets all criteria and has undergone testing and refinement, finalize the logo.

8. **Guidelines:** Create brand guidelines that detail logo usage, color codes, typography, and spacing rules to maintain consistency.

A well-crafted logo is a visual embodiment of a brand's identity and values. It has the power to evoke emotions, build trust, and leave a lasting impression. Effective logo design principles, combined with a thoughtful design process, contribute to the creation of iconic logos that stand the test of time.

Brand Consistency

Brand consistency is the bedrock of effective branding. It refers to the practice of maintaining a uniform and cohesive brand identity across all touchpoints and interactions with your audience.

This consistency ensures that your brand is easily recognizable, builds trust, and conveys a clear and memorable message.

Key Aspects of Brand Consistency:

1. **Visual Identity:** A consistent visual identity includes elements like logos, color palettes, typography, and imagery. These visual components should be used consistently in all brand materials, from websites and social media to printed materials and packaging.

2. **Tone and Messaging:** Consistency in the tone and messaging of your brand is vital. Whether your brand's voice is professional, casual, humorous, or authoritative, it should remain consistent across all communication channels.

3. **Brand Values:** The values and principles your brand stands for should be reflected consistently in your actions, content, and interactions with customers. Demonstrating a commitment to these values builds trust and credibility.

4. **Customer Experience:** Consistency in the customer experience, both online and offline, is crucial. From the moment a customer interacts with your brand to post-purchase interactions, the experience should align with your brand promise.

5. **Marketing Materials:** Whether it's digital marketing campaigns, print advertisements, or

social media posts, all marketing materials should adhere to your brand guidelines to maintain a cohesive look and feel.

The Benefits of Brand Consistency:

- **Recognition:** Consistent branding elements make your brand easily recognizable, even in a crowded marketplace.

- **Trust Building:** Brands that are consistent in their messaging and actions build trust with consumers, fostering loyalty.

- **Memorability:** A uniform brand identity makes your brand more memorable, increasing the likelihood that customers will remember and choose your products or services.

- **Professionalism:** Consistency conveys professionalism and reliability, which are crucial for attracting and retaining customers.

- **Clear Brand Message:** A consistent brand message helps consumers understand your brand's values, mission, and what it stands for.

Maintaining Brand Consistency:

1. **Brand Guidelines:** Develop comprehensive brand guidelines that outline how to use your brand's visual elements, tone, and messaging consistently.

These guidelines should be accessible to all team members and stakeholders.

2. **Training:** Ensure that employees and team members understand the importance of brand consistency and are trained to adhere to brand guidelines in their respective roles.

3. **Centralized Asset Management:** Use centralized digital asset management tools to store and distribute brand assets like logos, images, and templates.

4. **Regular Audits:** Periodically audit your brand materials and online presence to identify any inconsistencies and make necessary corrections.

5. **Feedback and Adaptation:** Collect feedback from customers and stakeholders to ensure that your brand remains aligned with their expectations. Be prepared to adapt if necessary.

Brand consistency is not a one-time effort but an ongoing commitment. It requires vigilance and dedication to ensure that every interaction with your brand reinforces its identity and values. By maintaining brand consistency, you can create a strong and lasting connection with your audience, fostering brand loyalty and recognition.

Case Studies in Branding

The world of branding is filled with success stories that demonstrate the power of effective brand strategies. In this section, we will explore some compelling case studies that highlight the importance of branding, showcasing how businesses and organizations have leveraged it to achieve remarkable success.

1. Coca-Cola: The Power of Brand Consistency

Objective: Coca-Cola, one of the world's most recognized brands, sought to maintain and reinforce its position as a global beverage leader.

Key Strategies:

- **Consistency:** Coca-Cola has maintained a consistent brand identity since its inception, from its iconic red and white logo to its timeless "Coca-Cola" script.

- **Emotionally Resonant Advertising:** Coca-Cola's advertising campaigns often focus on emotions and human connections, fostering a deep emotional connection with consumers.

- **Global Appeal:** Coca-Cola's brand is universally recognized, transcending cultural and linguistic barriers.

Results: Coca-Cola's unwavering commitment to brand consistency and emotional resonance has made it a symbol of happiness and unity worldwide, with its iconic red and white branding being instantly recognizable in nearly every corner of the globe.

2. Apple: Creating a Cult of Innovation

Objective: Apple aimed to position itself as a leader in innovation and design, catering to a loyal and passionate customer base.

Key Strategies:

- **Simplicity:** Apple's minimalist design philosophy is evident in its product design and packaging, conveying a sense of elegance and sophistication.

- **Product Integration:** Apple products seamlessly integrate with one another, creating an ecosystem that encourages brand loyalty.

- **Marketing Innovation:** Apple's marketing campaigns often focus on product features, design, and user experience, fostering a sense of anticipation and excitement.

Results: Apple has achieved cult-like status, with a dedicated fan base eagerly awaiting each product release. The brand's commitment to innovation and design excellence is synonymous with its identity.

3. Nike: Empowering Athletes Worldwide

Objective: Nike sought to empower athletes of all levels and establish itself as a symbol of athletic excellence.

Key Strategies:

- **Endorsements:** Nike collaborates with high-profile athletes and sports figures, associating the brand with excellence and achievement.

- **Just Do It:** The iconic "Just Do It" slogan encapsulates Nike's ethos of determination, pushing boundaries, and taking action.

- **Social Responsibility:** Nike's commitment to social and environmental responsibility resonates with consumers who align with these values.

Results: Nike's powerful brand encourages people to pursue their athletic goals and embodies the spirit of determination and achievement, making it a global symbol of sportswear excellence.

4. Airbnb: Creating a Sense of Belonging

Objective: Airbnb aimed to redefine travel by connecting travelers with unique, local accommodations while fostering a sense of belonging.

Key Strategies:

- **Community Building:** Airbnb fosters a sense of community among hosts and guests, emphasizing shared experiences and personal connections.

- **User-Generated Content:** User reviews and photos of accommodations provide authenticity and trustworthiness.

- **Belong Anywhere:** The "Belong Anywhere" tagline conveys the brand's mission of providing unique and personalized travel experiences.

Results: Airbnb's brand has disrupted the travel industry, emphasizing connection and community over traditional accommodations. It has created a global network of hosts and travelers who seek authentic experiences.

These case studies showcase the diversity of branding strategies and their impact on brand recognition, loyalty, and market leadership. Effective branding goes beyond logos and advertisements; it shapes the perception and identity of a business or organization, ultimately influencing consumer choices and loyalty.

Chapter 8: Visual Communication in Social Media

How Important?

Visual Communication in Social Media:

In the digital era, social media has transformed the way we connect, share information, and engage with content. It has become a dynamic and influential platform for individuals, businesses, and organizations to reach their target audiences. Visual communication plays a pivotal role in the success of social media strategies, and here's why it's so crucial:

1. **Immediate Impact:** Social media platforms are fast-paced environments where users scroll through content rapidly. Visual elements, such as images, videos, and infographics, have the power to grab attention instantly and convey messages quickly.

2. **Enhanced Engagement:** Visual content tends to generate higher levels of engagement compared to text-only posts. Whether it's a compelling image, an informative video, or an eye-catching infographic, visuals encourage likes, shares, comments, and click-throughs.

3. **Memorability:** People are more likely to remember content that includes visuals. Well-designed graphics, videos, and images leave a lasting impression and contribute to brand recall.

4. **Storytelling:** Visual communication enables storytelling in a concise and impactful manner. It allows brands and individuals to convey narratives, evoke emotions, and share experiences, making content more relatable and shareable.

5. **Cross-Platform Appeal:** Visual content can be adapted to suit various social media platforms, from image-centric platforms like Instagram and Pinterest to video-focused platforms like TikTok and YouTube. This adaptability ensures content resonates with specific platform audiences.

6. **Global Reach:** Visual content transcends language barriers, making it accessible and relatable to diverse global audiences. Brands can convey messages and connect with a global customer base through imagery and visuals.

7. **Brand Identity:** Consistent visual communication helps build and reinforce a brand's identity. Elements like color schemes, logos, and design styles create a cohesive and recognizable brand presence across social media channels.

8. **User-Generated Content:** Encouraging user-generated visual content, such as photos and videos shared by customers or followers, enhances authenticity and trust in your brand.

9. **Viral Potential:** Compelling visual content has the potential to go viral, spreading rapidly across

social media networks and reaching a broader audience than originally anticipated.

10. **Data Visualization:** Visual communication is effective for presenting data and complex information in an accessible and understandable format, fostering audience engagement with educational content.

In essence, visual communication is the linchpin of effective social media marketing and engagement. It not only captures attention but also conveys messages, builds brand recognition, and fosters deeper connections with audiences. As we explore the specific topic of "Crafting Engaging Social Media Graphics," we will delve into the strategies and principles that make visual content a potent tool in the social media landscape.

Crafting Engaging Social Media Graphics

In the digital age, social media has become a powerful platform for communication, marketing, and brand promotion. One of the most effective ways to capture attention and convey messages on social media is through visually engaging graphics. Crafting social media graphics requires a keen understanding of platform dynamics, design principles, and audience preferences.

Key Aspects of Crafting Engaging Social Media Graphics:

1. **Platform Compatibility:** Different social media platforms have varying image dimensions and requirements. Graphics should be tailored to fit each platform to ensure they display optimally.

2. **Visual Storytelling:** Social media graphics should tell a story or convey a message succinctly. The use of compelling visuals, icons, and text can effectively communicate information.

3. **Branding Elements:** Maintain consistency with your brand's visual identity, using colors, fonts, and logos in your social media graphics to reinforce brand recognition.

4. **Clarity and Simplicity:** Graphics should be clear and easy to understand at a glance. Avoid clutter and use concise text.

5. **Mobile Optimization:** With the majority of social media users accessing platforms on mobile devices, ensure that graphics are mobile-friendly and legible on small screens.

6. **Call-to-Action (CTA):** Encourage user engagement by incorporating clear CTAs in your graphics, prompting viewers to like, share, comment, or take a specific action.

7. **Visual Consistency:** Maintain a consistent visual style throughout your social media graphics. This consistency helps create a cohesive and memorable brand presence.

8. **A/B Testing:** Experiment with different graphic styles, layouts, and messaging to determine what resonates best with your audience. A/B testing can inform future graphic design choices.

The Power of Visual Content:

- **Attention-Grabbing:** Social media users scroll through a vast amount of content daily. Visually appealing graphics have a higher chance of capturing their attention amidst the noise.

- **Information Retention:** Visual content is often more memorable than text alone. People tend to retain information better when it's presented in a visually appealing manner.

- **Shareability:** Engaging graphics are more likely to be shared by users, extending the reach of your message.

- **Brand Recognition:** Consistent visual content strengthens brand recognition, making your posts instantly recognizable.

- **Emotion Elicitation:** Graphics can evoke emotions, whether it's humor, empathy, or excitement, leading to increased engagement.

Crafting engaging social media graphics is an art and science that requires a blend of design skills, knowledge of platform nuances, and an understanding of your target audience. Effective graphics have the power to amplify your brand's voice and message in the crowded and fast-paced world of social media.

Visual Content Strategy

In the realm of social media, content is king, and visual content reigns supreme. A well-defined visual content strategy is essential for businesses, organizations, and individuals aiming to make a meaningful impact on social media platforms. It involves careful planning, creation, and distribution of visual content to achieve specific goals and engage with the target audience effectively.

Key Components of a Visual Content Strategy:

1. **Audience Analysis:** Understand your target audience, their preferences, behavior, and the platforms they frequent. Tailor your visual content to resonate with this specific demographic.

2. **Content Goals:** Define clear objectives for your visual content. Are you aiming to increase brand awareness, drive website traffic, generate leads, or boost sales? Your goals will shape your content strategy.

3. **Content Types:** Identify the types of visual content that align with your goals and audience preferences. This can include images, videos, infographics, memes, user-generated content, and more.

4. **Consistency:** Maintain a consistent posting schedule to keep your audience engaged. Consistency builds anticipation and trust among followers.

5. **Platform Alignment:** Different social media platforms have varying content requirements and user behaviors. Tailor your visual content to fit each platform, optimizing it for platform-specific features and algorithms.

6. **Visual Branding:** Ensure that your visual content adheres to your brand's visual identity, including color schemes, fonts, logos, and design styles. Consistent branding helps strengthen brand recognition.

7. **Storytelling:** Effective visual content often tells a story or conveys a message. Craft narratives that resonate with your audience and elicit emotions.

8. **User Engagement:** Encourage user engagement by actively responding to comments, running contests or polls, and asking questions. Engaging with your audience fosters a sense of community.

9. **Analytics and Evaluation:** Regularly analyze the performance of your visual content. Metrics like engagement rate, reach, and conversion rates provide insights into what's working and what needs improvement.

10. **Adaptation:** Be flexible and open to adapting your visual content strategy based on audience feedback and changing trends. Continuously refine your strategy to stay relevant.

Benefits of a Visual Content Strategy:

- **Higher Engagement:** Visual content tends to generate more likes, shares, and comments compared to text-only content, increasing overall engagement.

- **Brand Recognition:** A consistent visual content strategy reinforces brand recognition, making your brand more memorable and trusted.

- **Audience Connection:** Visual content has the power to connect with audiences on an emotional level, fostering deeper connections and loyalty.

- **Expanded Reach:** Engaging visuals are more likely to be shared, expanding your content's reach beyond your immediate followers.

- **Enhanced Conversions:** Well-crafted visuals can drive user actions, such as clicking through to your website, signing up for newsletters, or making purchases.

- **Data-Driven Decisions:** By analyzing performance metrics, you can make data-driven decisions to optimize your visual content strategy for better results.

A well-executed visual content strategy can transform your social media presence from ordinary to extraordinary. It allows you to effectively communicate your message, engage with your audience, and achieve your social media marketing goals. In the ever-evolving landscape of social media, a thoughtful visual content strategy is your compass to navigate and succeed.

Case Studies in Social Media Campaigns

Social media has become a dynamic arena for marketing and communication, with countless successful campaigns serving as examples of the power of effective social media strategies. In this section, we will explore some compelling case studies that highlight innovative and impactful social media campaigns across various industries.

1. Airbnb's #LiveThere Campaign

Objective: Airbnb aimed to reposition itself as a platform for authentic travel experiences and foster stronger connections between hosts and guests.

Key Strategies:

- **User-Generated Content:** Airbnb encouraged hosts and guests to share their unique travel experiences on social media using the hashtag #LiveThere.

- **Emphasis on Local:** The campaign promoted exploring destinations like a local, rather than a tourist.

- **Storytelling:** Airbnb showcased real stories and experiences shared by its community members.

Results: The #LiveThere campaign successfully shifted Airbnb's image from a vacation rental platform to a provider of authentic, local experiences. User-generated content helped create a sense of trust and credibility, attracting more travelers seeking unique adventures.

2. Nike's "Dream Crazy" with Colin Kaepernick

Objective: Nike aimed to align itself with social issues and resonate with a younger, socially conscious audience.

Key Strategies:

- **Bold Endorsement:** Nike featured former NFL quarterback Colin Kaepernick, known for his activism, in its campaign.

- **Emotionally Charged Message:** The campaign embraced the tagline "Believe in something, even if it means sacrificing everything," addressing Kaepernick's activism.

- **Social Media Amplification:** Nike leveraged social media to amplify the campaign, sparking conversations and debates.

Results: Despite controversy, the "Dream Crazy" campaign garnered significant attention, increased brand mentions on social media, and resulted in higher sales and stock prices for Nike. It resonated with a younger demographic that valued brands taking a stand on social issues.

3. Wendy's "Nuggs for Carter" Campaign

Objective: Wendy's aimed to engage its Twitter audience and create buzz around its chicken nuggets.

Key Strategies:

- **Engagement Challenge:** Wendy's challenged a Twitter user named Carter Wilkerson to get 18 million retweets for a year's supply of chicken nuggets.

- **Hashtag Virality:** The campaign used the hashtag #NuggsForCarter to encourage retweets and generate social media buzz.

- **Playful Tone:** Wendy's engaged in playful banter with Carter and other users, creating a humorous and relatable tone.

Results: Carter's quest for free chicken nuggets went viral, receiving worldwide media coverage. Although he fell short of the 18 million retweets goal, the campaign was a massive success in terms of engagement, brand visibility, and social media mentions.

4. Coca-Cola's "Share a Coke" Campaign

Objective: Coca-Cola aimed to reconnect with its audience by personalizing its products and encouraging social sharing.

Key Strategies:

- **Personalized Bottles:** Coca-Cola replaced its logo with popular names, encouraging consumers to "Share a Coke" with friends and loved ones.

- **User-Generated Content:** The campaign invited consumers to share photos of themselves with personalized bottles on social media using the hashtag #ShareACoke.

- **Inclusivity:** The campaign featured a diverse range of names and encouraged people to find their name or share a Coke with someone special.

Results: The "Share a Coke" campaign revitalized Coca-Cola's brand and generated significant user-generated content on social media. It encouraged sharing and engagement, making it one of the most successful marketing campaigns in recent years.

These case studies illustrate the diverse strategies employed by brands to leverage the power of social media. Whether it's fostering community engagement, addressing social issues, or personalizing products, social media campaigns can have a profound impact on brand visibility, engagement, and even sales. Successful campaigns often resonate with audiences on a personal and emotional level, driving meaningful interactions and conversations.

Chapter 9: Visual Communication in Presentations

Presentations are a ubiquitous means of conveying information, ideas, and messages across various domains, from business and education to public speaking and conferences. Visual communication plays a pivotal role in the effectiveness of presentations. Here's why it's crucial:

1. **Enhanced Comprehension:** Visuals, such as diagrams, charts, and images, aid in clarifying complex concepts and data. They make information more accessible and understandable to the audience.

2. **Retention:** Studies show that people remember information better when it's presented with visuals. Visuals create a lasting impact and improve information recall.

3. **Engagement:** Visual elements capture the audience's attention and maintain their interest throughout the presentation. This engagement is vital for conveying your message effectively.

4. **Storytelling:** Visuals are powerful storytelling tools. They can evoke emotions, illustrate narratives, and make your presentation more compelling and relatable.

5. **Simplicity:** Visuals can simplify complex topics, distilling them into digestible and memorable components. This simplification aids in audience comprehension.

6. **Universal Language:** Visuals transcend language barriers, making them suitable for international audiences and diverse cultural settings.

7. **Professionalism:** Well-designed visuals convey professionalism and attention to detail, enhancing the overall quality of your presentation.

8. **Persuasion:** Visuals can be persuasive, supporting your arguments and influencing your audience's opinions and decisions.

Components of Effective Visual Communication in Presentations:

1. **Clarity:** Visuals should be clear and unambiguous, conveying information without confusion. Avoid clutter and unnecessary complexity.

2. **Relevance:** Visuals should align with the content and the message you're conveying. They should enhance, not distract from, your presentation.

3. **Consistency:** Maintain a consistent visual style throughout your presentation, using the same color scheme, fonts, and design elements. Consistency reinforces your brand or message.

4. **Balance:** Distribute visuals evenly across your presentation to maintain a harmonious flow. Avoid overloading slides with text or visuals.

5. **Engagement:** Use visuals that engage the audience emotionally and intellectually. Storytelling visuals, relatable images, and compelling graphics can achieve this.

6. **Accessibility:** Ensure that your visuals are accessible to all audience members, including those with visual impairments. Use alt text for images and ensure readability.

7. **Interactivity:** In some presentations, interactive visuals, such as clickable infographics or embedded videos, can enhance engagement and understanding.

8. **Data Visualization:** When presenting data, use charts, graphs, and visual representations to make the data more comprehensible and persuasive.

9. **Visual Hierarchy:** Use visual hierarchy principles to guide the audience's attention to key points and information in your presentation.

Visual communication in presentations is not merely about adding images to slides; it's about creating a compelling and effective narrative. Well-designed visuals, combined with a thoughtful presentation structure and delivery, can elevate your message and leave a lasting impression on your audience. In the subsequent sections of this chapter, we'll delve deeper into the strategies and case studies that exemplify the impact of visual communication in presentations.

Designing Effective Slides

Effective slide design is a cornerstone of compelling presentations. Well-designed slides enhance audience engagement, comprehension, and retention of information. Here's why designing effective slides is crucial:

1. **Visual Appeal:** Professionally designed slides capture the audience's attention and convey a sense of expertise and professionalism.

2. **Clarity:** Well-structured slides present information clearly and concisely, preventing confusion and ensuring that the audience grasps key points.

3. **Focus:** Effective slide design directs the audience's attention to the most important information, helping them stay engaged and retain critical details.

4. **Flow:** Thoughtful slide layout and organization create a logical flow that guides the audience through the presentation seamlessly.

5. **Emphasis:** Strategic use of visuals, typography, and color can highlight key takeaways and support the speaker's message.

6. **Accessibility:** Considerate design choices ensure that all audience members, including those with

visual impairments, can access and understand the content.

Key Principles for Designing Effective Slides:

1. **Simplicity:** Avoid clutter and keep slides uncluttered. Use concise text, simple graphics, and ample white space.

2. **Consistency:** Maintain a consistent design theme throughout your presentation. Use the same fonts, colors, and design elements on all slides.

3. **Legibility:** Ensure that text is legible from a distance. Choose readable fonts and use appropriate font sizes.

4. **Visuals:** Incorporate relevant visuals, such as images, diagrams, and charts, to illustrate key points. Ensure that visuals enhance understanding.

5. **Hierarchy:** Use visual hierarchy to emphasize important information. Larger fonts, bold text, and color contrast can help create hierarchy.

6. **Alignment:** Align elements on the slide for a clean and organized look. Consistent alignment helps maintain visual order.

7. **Contrast:** Use contrast in color and font to draw attention to specific elements. High contrast can make important information stand out.

8. **Limited Bullet Points:** Avoid excessive bullet points. Instead, use short, impactful phrases or even single keywords to convey information.

9. **Minimal Text:** Keep text minimal and use bullet points sparingly. Use visuals and the speaker's narrative to expand on key points.

10. **Whitespace:** Embrace whitespace to give your content room to breathe. It reduces visual clutter and makes slides more visually appealing.

Interactive Elements: Depending on the platform and audience, consider incorporating interactive elements like clickable links, buttons, or multimedia to engage the audience and enhance the presentation's interactivity.

Effective slide design complements the content and enhances the overall impact of your presentation. It ensures that your audience remains engaged, retains information, and leaves with a clear understanding of your message. In the subsequent sections, we'll delve into specific strategies for designing slides that captivate and inform your audience effectively.

Storytelling with Visuals

Storytelling is a powerful technique in presentations, and when combined with visuals, it becomes even more impactful. Storytelling with visuals involves using images, graphics, and multimedia elements to weave a compelling narrative that resonates with your audience. Here's why storytelling with visuals is essential:

1. **Engagement:** Stories are inherently engaging. When you tell a story with visuals, it captivates your audience's attention and keeps them interested in your presentation.

2. **Emotion:** Visual storytelling has the ability to evoke emotions. Well-chosen visuals can make your audience feel connected, empathetic, and emotionally invested in your message.

3. **Clarity:** Stories provide context and structure to information. Visuals enhance clarity by illustrating and reinforcing key points within the narrative.

4. **Memorability:** Stories are more memorable than facts or data alone. Visuals associated with your story create a lasting impression in your audience's minds.

5. **Alignment:** A well-crafted visual story aligns with your presentation's overall message and helps convey complex ideas in a relatable manner.

Effective Strategies for Storytelling with Visuals:

1. **Narrative Arc:** Structure your presentation like a story, with a clear beginning, middle, and end. Introduce a problem or challenge, present a solution or resolution, and use visuals to support each stage.

2. **Character and Conflict:** If applicable, include relatable characters and conflicts in your story. Visuals of people, whether photographs or illustrations, can add a human element to your narrative.

3. **Visual Metaphors:** Use visual metaphors to convey abstract concepts or ideas. For example, a puzzle piece fitting into a larger puzzle can represent collaboration or unity.

4. **Sequential Visuals:** If your story involves a process or progression, use sequential visuals or infographics to illustrate each step.

5. **Emotional Appeal:** Select visuals that elicit emotions related to your story. Happiness, empathy, surprise, or even humor can enhance the impact of your narrative.

6. **Contrast and Transformation:** Visuals that show a contrast or transformation can emphasize the evolution of your story. This could be a "before and after" comparison or a journey of growth.

7. **Symbolism:** Employ symbolic visuals that represent overarching themes or messages in your story. These symbols can serve as recurring motifs throughout your presentation.

8. **Timing:** Coordinate the timing of your visuals with your spoken narrative. Reveal visuals at strategic moments to enhance the storytelling experience.

9. **Consistency:** Maintain a consistent visual style throughout your story to ensure cohesiveness and reinforce your message.

10. **Audience Engagement:** Encourage audience engagement by asking questions or prompting reflections related to your story. Visuals can also be used for interactive elements.

Effective storytelling with visuals goes beyond mere decoration; it weaves a narrative that connects with your audience on a deeper level. It allows you to convey not just information but also emotions, experiences, and insights. In the subsequent sections, we'll explore case studies that demonstrate the power of visual storytelling in presentations.

Case Studies in Presentation Design

Effective presentation design can be a game-changer when it comes to delivering impactful messages and engaging your audience. Let's delve into some case studies that showcase exceptional presentation design and the positive outcomes it can achieve:

1. Steve Jobs' iPhone Launch Presentation:

Objective: Steve Jobs aimed to introduce the world to the first iPhone, a groundbreaking product that would redefine the smartphone industry.

Key Design Elements:

- **Visual Simplicity:** Jobs used clean, uncluttered slides with minimal text, focusing on high-resolution images of the iPhone.

- **Dramatic Reveals:** He strategically unveiled the iPhone's features one by one, creating anticipation and excitement.

- **Engaging Visuals:** The presentation included videos, graphics, and images that showcased the iPhone's design and functionality.

Results: The iPhone launch presentation is legendary for its impact. Jobs' effective use of visual design and storytelling left the audience in awe. It contributed significantly to the iPhone's successful launch and its lasting impact on the tech industry.

2. TED Talks - Various Speakers:

Objective: TED Talks aim to share "ideas worth spreading" with a global audience.

Key Design Elements:

- **Consistent Format:** TED Talks maintain a consistent format with large, high-quality visuals and minimal text.

- **Engaging Visuals:** Speakers use compelling images, videos, and slides to enhance their narratives.

- **Visual Reinforcement:** Visuals are synchronized with the speaker's words, reinforcing key points.

Results: TED Talks have become synonymous with impactful presentations. The consistent and visually engaging design plays a crucial role in holding the audience's attention and facilitating the spread of innovative ideas.

3. NASA's "Journey to Mars" Presentation:

Objective: NASA aimed to inform the public and stakeholders about its ambitious plans to send humans to Mars.

Key Design Elements:

- **Stunning Visuals:** The presentation featured breathtaking images of Mars, spacecraft, and astronauts.

- **Infographics:** Infographics were used to simplify complex concepts, such as spacecraft trajectories.

- **Emotional Appeal:** The presentation included visuals of astronauts' families, creating an emotional connection to the mission.

Results: NASA's "Journey to Mars" presentation effectively conveyed the agency's vision and generated public excitement and support for its Mars exploration plans.

4. Duarte's Work with Silicon Valley Executives:

Objective: Duarte, a presentation design agency, collaborates with Silicon Valley executives to enhance their pitch presentations.

Key Design Elements:

- **Narrative Structure:** Duarte helps executives craft compelling stories that resonate with investors and stakeholders.

- **Visual Impact:** High-quality visuals, animations, and infographics are used to illustrate key points.

- **Consistency:** Duarte ensures a consistent visual identity throughout the presentation.

Results: Duarte's collaboration has led to successful funding rounds, partnerships, and business expansions for Silicon Valley companies, demonstrating the impact of effective presentation design on business outcomes.

These case studies highlight the transformative power of presentation design. From product launches to TED Talks, well-designed presentations can inform, inspire, and drive action. They demonstrate that visual communication is not merely an accessory to presentations; it is a fundamental tool for achieving communication objectives and making lasting impressions.

Chapter 10: Visual Communication in Data Visualization

Data visualization is the art and science of presenting data in a visual format that is easily understandable and meaningful to the audience. Visual communication is integral to effective data visualization, and here's why it holds immense importance:

1. **Clarity and Comprehension:** Visualizing data makes complex information more accessible. Visual elements like charts, graphs, and maps simplify data interpretation, allowing the audience to grasp insights quickly.

2. **Insight Discovery:** Well-designed visualizations can reveal patterns, trends, and correlations within data that may not be apparent in raw numbers. They enable data-driven decision-making.

3. **Memory Retention:** People remember information better when it's presented visually. Visual data representations create memorable impressions, aiding in knowledge retention.

4. **Universal Language:** Visual data transcends language barriers, making it universally understandable. This is particularly important in today's globalized world.

5. **Engagement:** Visual data engages the audience more effectively than rows of numbers or lengthy reports. Engaged viewers are more likely to explore the data and draw conclusions.

6. **Storytelling:** Visualizations can tell compelling data stories. They guide the audience through the data, helping them connect with the narrative and understand the context.

Key Principles for Visual Communication in Data Visualization:

1. **Simplicity:** Keep visualizations simple and focused on the data's core message. Avoid clutter and unnecessary embellishments.

2. **Relevance:** Ensure that your visualizations directly relate to your data and the message you want to convey. Irrelevant visuals can confuse the audience.

3. **Accuracy:** Visualizations should accurately represent the data. Misleading or inaccurate visualizations can lead to incorrect conclusions.

4. **Interactivity:** Depending on the platform and audience, consider adding interactive elements to allow viewers to explore the data further.

5. **Consistency:** Maintain a consistent design style throughout your visualizations, using the same colors, fonts, and labeling conventions.

6. **Accessibility:** Ensure that visualizations are accessible to all viewers, including those with disabilities. Use clear labels, alt text for images, and consider color contrast.

7. **Engaging Story:** Develop a narrative or story around your data that guides viewers through the visualization and helps them understand its significance.

Benefits of Effective Data Visualization:

- **Informed Decision-Making:** Visualized data provides decision-makers with clear insights, helping them make informed choices.

- **Effective Communication:** Data visualizations enable you to communicate complex data to a broad audience in an understandable manner.

- **Efficiency:** Visual data can be processed more quickly than text or numerical data, saving time for both presenters and viewers.

- **Data Exploration:** Interactive visualizations allow viewers to explore data on their terms, fostering a deeper understanding.

- **Problem-Solving:** Visualizations can reveal problems or opportunities that may not be evident in the raw data, supporting problem-solving efforts.

In the subsequent sections of this chapter, we will explore specific strategies for effective data presentation, the use of infographics and charts, and examine case studies that exemplify the impact of visual communication in data visualization. Data visualization is a powerful tool for unlocking the insights hidden within data and communicating those insights effectively.

Effective Data Presentation

Effective data presentation is about transforming raw data into a format that is easily comprehensible, meaningful, and actionable. Whether you're addressing a boardroom, a classroom, or a broader audience, how you present data can greatly influence how it is understood and used. Here are key considerations for effective data presentation:

1. **Audience Understanding:** Tailor your data presentation to your audience's level of expertise. Use terminology and visualizations that are appropriate for their background and knowledge.

2. **Clarity of Message:** Start with a clear message or takeaway you want to convey. What story does the data tell, and what action do you want the audience to take?

3. **Appropriate Visualization:** Choose the right type of data visualization for your dataset and message. Options include bar charts, line graphs, scatter plots, pie charts, and more. The choice depends on

the data's nature and the insights you want to highlight.

4. **Simplicity:** Simplify your data visuals. Avoid unnecessary complexity, decorative elements, and distractions. Focus on the key data points that support your message.

5. **Annotations and Labels:** Label your data points and use annotations to provide context or highlight key findings. Ensure that axes, legends, and labels are clearly legible.

6. **Consistency:** Maintain consistency in style, colors, and fonts throughout your data presentation. A consistent design helps the audience focus on the data, not on deciphering the visuals.

7. **Engagement:** Engage your audience with interactive elements when appropriate. Interactive visualizations allow viewers to explore data and uncover insights on their own.

8. **Storytelling:** Present data as part of a narrative. Begin with an introduction, present the data's main points, and conclude with a summary or call to action. Storytelling helps the audience connect with the data emotionally and intellectually.

9. **Accessibility:** Ensure that your data presentation is accessible to all viewers, including those with disabilities. Use clear alt text for images, provide

transcripts for audio content, and consider color contrast for readability.

10. **Practice and Rehearsal:** Practice your data presentation multiple times to ensure smooth delivery. Be prepared to answer questions and provide additional context if needed.

Visual Communication Tools: Various tools and software are available to assist in creating effective data presentations. These tools offer features for data visualization, storytelling, and interactivity. Some popular options include Microsoft PowerPoint, Tableau, Google Data Studio, and Adobe Illustrator.

Remember that the goal of effective data presentation is not only to inform but also to inspire action. Whether you're presenting sales figures, research findings, or survey results, the way you present the data can influence decision-making, persuade stakeholders, and drive change. In the subsequent sections of this chapter, we'll explore the use of infographics and charts as powerful tools for presenting data in an engaging and understandable manner.

Infographics and Charts

Infographics and charts are invaluable tools in data visualization and communication. They simplify complex information, making it more accessible and engaging for your audience. Here's why infographics and charts are essential:

Infographics:

1. **Visual Storytelling:** Infographics combine text, images, and graphics to tell a visual story. They capture the audience's attention and convey information in a narrative format.

2. **Complex Data Simplified:** Infographics distill complex data into digestible and visually appealing formats. They present key insights and statistics in an easily understandable manner.

3. **Retention:** Visual content, such as infographics, is more memorable than text alone. Viewers retain information presented in an infographic more effectively.

4. **Versatility:** Infographics can be used across various platforms, from presentations and reports to social media and websites. They adapt to different communication needs.

5. **Brand Identity:** Infographics offer opportunities for branding and customization. You can

incorporate your organization's colors, fonts, and logos to reinforce your brand identity.

Charts:

1. **Data Visualization:** Charts are designed specifically for data representation. They provide a visual representation of numerical information, making trends and patterns evident.

2. **Comparison:** Charts facilitate comparisons between data points, enabling viewers to analyze relationships and differences more effectively.

3. **Data Accuracy:** Well-constructed charts accurately represent data, reducing the risk of misinterpretation or misunderstanding.

4. **Decision Support:** Charts aid in decision-making by providing a visual summary of data, helping stakeholders quickly grasp key information.

5. **Variety:** Various chart types, such as bar charts, line graphs, pie charts, and scatter plots, can be chosen to match the data and message requirements.

Effective Use of Infographics and Charts:

1. **Relevance:** Ensure that the choice of infographics or charts aligns with your data and message. Use infographics for storytelling and charts for precise data representation.

2. **Simplicity:** Keep both infographics and charts simple and uncluttered. Eliminate unnecessary elements that can distract from the main message.

3. **Color and Contrast:** Use color strategically to highlight key points, but avoid overwhelming viewers with excessive colors. Ensure proper contrast for readability.

4. **Labels and Titles:** Include clear labels, titles, and legends to guide viewers through your infographics and charts. Labels provide context and understanding.

5. **Consistency:** Maintain consistency in design and style across all infographics and charts in your presentation. Consistency enhances visual coherence.

6. **Interactivity:** Depending on the platform, consider adding interactive elements to charts, allowing viewers to explore data points further.

Infographics and charts are versatile tools that transform data into meaningful visuals. When used effectively, they enhance communication, engage your audience, and facilitate data-driven decision-making. In the subsequent sections, we will explore case studies that showcase the impact of infographics and charts in various contexts.

Case Studies in Data Visualization

Let's explore real-world case studies that demonstrate the power of data visualization in various domains and the positive outcomes it can achieve:

1. John Snow's Cholera Map (1854):

Objective: Physician John Snow's famous cholera map aimed to understand the cholera outbreak in London's Soho district and identify its source.

Key Data Visualization Element:

- **Geospatial Mapping:** Snow plotted cholera cases on a map, revealing a cluster around a specific water pump.

Results: Snow's data visualization provided compelling evidence that contaminated water from the Broad Street pump was the source of the cholera outbreak. This pioneering use of data visualization helped advance the field of epidemiology.

2. The New York Times' COVID-19 Tracking:

Objective: During the COVID-19 pandemic, The New York Times aimed to provide the public with accurate and up-to-date information on cases, deaths, and vaccination progress.

Key Data Visualization Elements:

- **Interactive Maps:** The Times used interactive maps to show COVID-19 trends by state and county.

- **Data Dashboards:** Dashboards displayed key metrics, such as daily cases, deaths, and vaccination rates.

- **Visual Timelines:** Timelines illustrated the progression of the pandemic.

Results: The Times' data visualizations helped the public track the pandemic's impact and make informed decisions about safety measures and vaccinations.

3. Gapminder's Global Health Visualizations:

Objective: Gapminder, led by Hans Rosling, aimed to challenge misconceptions about global health and development using data.

Key Data Visualization Elements:

- **Animated Bubble Charts:** Animated bubble charts showed the correlation between income, life expectancy, and population size in various countries.

- **Time Series Graphs:** Time series graphs revealed changes in health indicators over time.

Results: Gapminder's data visualizations altered public perceptions about global health and highlighted the progress achieved in many countries, leading to more informed discussions on development issues.

4. NASA's Mars Rover Data Visualization:

Objective: NASA's Mars rover missions required effective data visualization to understand geological and atmospheric data from the Red Planet.

Key Data Visualization Elements:

- **3D Terrain Models:** 3D models of Martian terrain aided in rover navigation.

- **Spectrograms:** Spectrograms displayed the composition of Martian rocks and soil.

Results: NASA's data visualizations supported mission success by helping scientists analyze data remotely and make informed decisions about rover activities.

5. Financial Times' Visualizations of Economic Data:

Objective: The Financial Times uses data visualizations to provide readers with insights into economic trends and market data.

Key Data Visualization Elements:

- **Stock Market Charts:** Interactive charts track stock market indices and individual stock performance.

- **Economic Indicators:** Visualizations display data on unemployment rates, GDP growth, and inflation.

Results: The Financial Times' data visualizations empower readers with tools to analyze economic data and make informed financial decisions.

These case studies demonstrate how effective data visualization can illuminate patterns, inform decisions, and convey complex information. Whether it's understanding disease outbreaks, challenging perceptions, exploring other planets, or analyzing financial markets, data visualization is a powerful tool for turning data into actionable insights.

Chapter 11: Visual Communication in Film and Multimedia

Visual communication is at the heart of the film and multimedia industry, shaping how stories are told and experiences are crafted. It plays a pivotal role in engaging audiences, conveying emotions, and delivering messages effectively. Here's why visual communication is of paramount importance in the realm of film and multimedia:

1. **Emotional Impact:** Visuals have a profound ability to evoke emotions and connect with viewers on a visceral level. Facial expressions, scenery, and cinematography all contribute to the emotional resonance of a film or multimedia project.

2. **Storytelling:** Visuals are a primary vehicle for storytelling. They provide context, set the mood, and help narrate the plot. Effective visual storytelling immerses the audience in the narrative.

3. **Engagement:** Visual elements, including graphics, animations, and special effects, capture and sustain the audience's attention. Engaged viewers are more likely to absorb the message or story being conveyed.

4. **Information Conveyance:** In multimedia presentations and documentaries, visual aids such as charts, graphs, and animations can simplify complex concepts and make information more digestible.

5. **Branding and Identity:** Visual communication plays a critical role in establishing and reinforcing brand identity. Logos, color schemes, and design elements contribute to brand recognition.

6. **Creativity and Innovation:** The film and multimedia industry thrives on creativity and innovation in visual storytelling. Directors, cinematographers, and animators continually push the boundaries of what's visually possible.

Key Aspects of Visual Communication in Film and Multimedia:

1. **Cinematography:** Cinematographers use camera techniques, framing, and lighting to create visually compelling scenes. Camera movements and angles can convey mood and perspective.

2. **Visual Effects:** Visual effects artists employ cutting-edge technology to add realism or fantasy to films and multimedia. From CGI creatures to explosive action sequences, visual effects enhance storytelling.

3. **Motion Graphics:** Motion graphics combine visual design and animation to convey information dynamically. They are often used in titles, lower thirds, and explanatory videos.

4. **Editing:** Editors shape the narrative through the selection and arrangement of visual and audio

elements. The pacing of edits can influence the viewer's emotional response.

5. **Sound and Music:** Although not visual in nature, sound and music are integral to multimedia and film. They complement visuals, create atmosphere, and heighten emotions.

6. **Interactive Multimedia:** In interactive multimedia, visual communication extends to user interfaces, gaming graphics, and interactive storytelling. User engagement relies on visual design and interactivity.

The Power of Visual Communication in Film and Multimedia:

- **Audience Connection:** Visual communication facilitates a deep connection between creators and audiences. It allows filmmakers and multimedia producers to convey their messages, ideas, and stories in ways that resonate and leave a lasting impact.

- **Immersion:** Effective visual communication immerses viewers in the world of the film or multimedia experience. It transports them to different realms, whether they're exploring a fantastical universe or gaining insight into a real-world issue.

- **Education and Information:** In educational multimedia, visual communication simplifies complex concepts, making learning more engaging and accessible. It is a key tool in conveying information effectively.

- **Artistic Expression:** Visual communication in film and multimedia is a canvas for artistic expression. Filmmakers, animators, and designers use their creativity to captivate and inspire.

In the chapters that follow, we will delve into specific aspects of visual communication in film and multimedia, including the role of visual effects, the art of motion graphics, and case studies that showcase the impact of visual storytelling in this dynamic field.

Visual Effects and Storytelling

Visual effects (VFX) play a pivotal role in modern filmmaking and multimedia storytelling. They have revolutionized the way stories are told on screen, expanding the possibilities of what can be imagined and presented to audiences. Here's how visual effects intersect with storytelling:

Enhancing Immersion:

- Visual effects transport viewers to fantastical worlds, historical settings, or futuristic landscapes, enhancing immersion. They create environments that may not exist in reality but are crucial to the narrative.

Creating Spectacle:

- Visual effects enable filmmakers to bring larger-than-life spectacles to the screen. Whether it's epic battles, mind-bending science fiction, or awe-inspiring creatures, VFX make the extraordinary believable.

Conveying Emotion:

- Visual effects can evoke powerful emotions. From the fear instilled by a menacing monster to the wonder inspired by otherworldly beauty, VFX contribute to the emotional impact of a story.

Expanding Creative Boundaries:

- VFX push creative boundaries by allowing filmmakers to explore concepts and visuals that were once impossible to achieve. This fosters innovation and artistic expression.

Seamless Integration:

- The best VFX seamlessly integrate with live-action footage and practical effects. When done right, viewers may not even realize the extent of visual effects used in a film or multimedia project.

Visual Effects in Different Genres:

1. **Science Fiction and Fantasy:** Visual effects are integral to creating futuristic worlds, alien landscapes, and magical realms in science fiction and fantasy genres. They enable the portrayal of advanced technology, interstellar journeys, and supernatural phenomena.

2. **Superhero Films:** Superhero films rely heavily on VFX to bring iconic characters and their superpowers to life. They showcase epic battles, transformations, and breathtaking stunts.

3. **Historical Epics:** Visual effects can transport viewers to historical periods with meticulous attention to detail. They recreate ancient civilizations, epic battles, and architectural wonders.

4. **Horror:** Horror films use VFX to create terrifying creatures, eerie atmospheres, and gruesome effects that intensify scares and suspense.

5. **Animation:** Animation, whether 2D or 3D, is a form of visual effects in itself. Animated films leverage VFX techniques to craft dynamic and visually stunning narratives.

Challenges and Considerations:

- While VFX offer immense creative possibilities, their successful implementation requires meticulous planning, coordination, and budgeting.

- Balancing practical effects with digital enhancements is crucial to maintain authenticity and believability.

- VFX artists must stay at the forefront of technology to deliver cutting-edge effects.

- The visual effects industry faces ethical questions about the extent to which reality can be altered through manipulation.

Visual effects have transformed storytelling, making it possible to realize visions that were once confined to the realm of imagination. They continue to shape the way narratives are crafted, providing filmmakers and multimedia creators with an expansive toolkit for storytelling. In the subsequent sections, we will explore the art of motion graphics and examine case studies that highlight the impact of visual effects in film and multimedia.

Motion Graphics

Motion graphics are a dynamic and versatile form of visual communication that combines graphic design, animation, and storytelling to convey information, engage audiences, and enhance multimedia presentations. Here's why motion graphics are essential in the world of film and multimedia:

1. Dynamic Visual Storytelling:

- Motion graphics add movement and fluidity to visual narratives, making them more engaging and captivating.

- They can simplify complex concepts by breaking them down into animated sequences, aiding in comprehension.

2. Information Visualization:

- Motion graphics excel at presenting data and information in an easily digestible format. They transform static charts and graphs into dynamic, animated visuals.

- Infographics, explainer videos, and educational animations are all examples of motion graphics used for information dissemination.

3. Branding and Identity:

- Organizations use motion graphics to reinforce their brand identity. Animated logos, intros, and outros leave a memorable impression on viewers.

- Consistent motion graphics across multimedia content strengthen brand recognition.

4. Engagement and Interactivity:

- Motion graphics can be interactive, allowing users to engage with content. This interactivity fosters a deeper connection between audiences and the material.

- In presentations and e-learning modules, interactive motion graphics enhance user engagement.

5. Visual Appeal:

- The dynamic nature of motion graphics adds visual appeal to multimedia content. They bring a sense of liveliness and vibrancy to videos, websites, and presentations.

Key Elements of Motion Graphics:

1. **Typography:** Text animation is a fundamental aspect of motion graphics. Kinetic typography uses movement to convey messages creatively.

2. **Illustrations and Icons:** Graphic elements such as icons, symbols, and illustrations are often animated to reinforce concepts or narratives.

3. **Transitions:** Motion graphics are used for smooth transitions between scenes or ideas, creating a cohesive flow in multimedia presentations.

4. **Timing and Rhythm:** Timing is crucial in motion graphics. Proper pacing and rhythm in animations can evoke emotions and maintain viewer interest.

5. **Color and Composition:** Effective use of color and composition enhances the visual impact of motion graphics. Color schemes and layout contribute to the overall design.

6. **Sound Design:** Sound effects and music synchronize with motion graphics to create a multisensory experience.

Applications of Motion Graphics:

1. **Explainer Videos:** Motion graphics are commonly used in explainer videos to simplify complex concepts and introduce products or services.

2. **Educational Content:** Motion graphics enhance e-learning materials, making lessons more engaging and memorable.

3. **Advertising and Marketing:** Animated advertisements and promotional videos grab attention and convey messages effectively.

4. **Presentations:** In business and academia, motion graphics improve the visual appeal and clarity of presentations.

5. **Entertainment:** Motion graphics are integral to film and television, enriching title sequences, visual effects, and animated sequences.

6. **User Interfaces:** Animated elements in user interfaces enhance user experience and guide interactions.

The power of motion graphics lies in their ability to blend creativity with information dissemination. They transform static content into dynamic, memorable experiences, making them a valuable asset in film, multimedia, marketing, education, and various other fields. In the sections that follow, we will explore case studies that exemplify the impact of motion graphics in different contexts.

Case Studies in Film and Multimedia

Let's delve into real-world case studies that showcase the impactful use of visual communication in film and multimedia projects. These examples demonstrate how visual storytelling, visual effects, and motion graphics contribute to the success and resonance of multimedia narratives:

1. "The Lord of the Rings" Trilogy (Film):

Objective: To bring J.R.R. Tolkien's epic fantasy world to life on the big screen.

Visual Communication Elements:

- **Visual Effects:** Extensive use of visual effects to create mythical creatures, epic battles, and fantastical landscapes.

- **Cinematography:** Sweeping shots of New Zealand's natural beauty enhanced the sense of Middle-earth.

- **Motion Graphics:** Elaborate title sequences with intricate animations introduced each film.

Results: The trilogy's masterful use of visual communication elements set a new standard for fantasy filmmaking. It immersed viewers in a richly detailed world, earning critical acclaim and numerous awards.

2. "Planet Earth" (Television Documentary Series):

Objective: To showcase the diversity of Earth's ecosystems and wildlife.

Visual Communication Elements:

- **Cinematography:** Stunning high-definition footage captured Earth's natural beauty and wildlife behavior.

- **Visual Effects:** Used minimally to enhance certain sequences, such as time-lapse photography.

Results: "Planet Earth" wowed audiences with its breathtaking visuals and compelling storytelling. It raised awareness of environmental issues and garnered widespread acclaim for its cinematography.

3. "The Wall Street Journal" Interactive Graphics (Online Multimedia):

Objective: To explain complex economic and financial concepts to a general audience.

Visual Communication Elements:

- **Motion Graphics:** Animated infographics and explanatory videos simplified economic data and trends.

- **Interactive Charts:** Users could interact with dynamic charts and explore data on the website.

Results: The Wall Street Journal's use of visual communication in multimedia content made financial news more accessible and engaging. Interactive graphics empowered users to understand economic topics better.

4. "TED-Ed" Educational Videos (Online Education):

Objective: To deliver educational content in an engaging and accessible format.

Visual Communication Elements:

- **Motion Graphics:** Animated characters and visuals accompanied educational narratives.

- **Interactive Elements:** Quizzes and supplementary materials enhanced the learning experience.

Results: TED-Ed's educational videos leveraged motion graphics and interactivity to make complex topics enjoyable and understandable for learners of all ages.

5. "Black Mirror: Bandersnatch" (Interactive Film):

Objective: To create an interactive narrative experience, allowing viewers to make choices that impact the story.

Visual Communication Elements:

- **Interactive Storytelling:** Viewers made decisions at key points, shaping the narrative's outcome.

- **Cinematography:** Seamlessly integrated with the interactive storytelling to maintain continuity.

Results: "Black Mirror: Bandersnatch" was praised for its innovative approach to storytelling, blending film and interactivity. It pushed the boundaries of traditional narrative forms.

These case studies illustrate the versatility and impact of visual communication in film and multimedia. From epic fantasy worlds to educational content and interactive storytelling, visual elements play a vital role in captivating audiences, conveying information, and pushing the boundaries of creative expression in multimedia projects.

Chapter 12: Visual Communication Ethics

Ethical Considerations in Visual Design

Ethical considerations in visual design are essential to maintain trust, integrity, and responsibility in communication. Visual designers must be mindful of ethical principles to ensure their work aligns with ethical standards. Here are some key aspects of ethical considerations in visual design:

1. **Accuracy and Truthfulness:** Visual designers should strive for accuracy in depicting information and avoid misrepresenting facts or data. The use of misleading or fabricated visuals should be avoided at all costs.

2. **Respect for Privacy:** Designers must respect individuals' privacy rights when using images, personal data, or any content that may infringe on privacy.

3. **Cultural Sensitivity:** Cultural nuances and sensitivities should be respected in visual design to avoid cultural appropriation or insensitivity.

4. **Inclusivity and Diversity:** Visual designs should aim to be inclusive and represent diverse perspectives, backgrounds, and experiences.

5. **Transparency:** Designers should be transparent about the sources of their visuals and give credit when using third-party content.

6. **Avoiding Harm:** Visuals should not perpetuate harm, discrimination, or stereotypes. Designers should consider the potential impact of their visuals on society.

7. **Consent:** Obtaining proper consent for the use of images, likenesses, or any personal data is critical. Without consent, using such visuals can breach privacy and ethical standards.

8. **Environmental Responsibility:** Designers should consider the environmental impact of their work, including the use of resources, energy, and sustainable design practices.

Ethical considerations in visual design guide responsible and conscientious design practices. They ensure that visuals are not only visually appealing but also morally sound and aligned with ethical values.

In the subsequent sections, we will delve into avoiding misleading visuals and explore case studies that illuminate ethical dilemmas in visual communication.

Avoiding Misleading Visuals

Avoiding misleading visuals is a fundamental ethical principle in visual communication.

Misleading visuals can distort facts, deceive audiences, and erode trust. Visual designers and communicators should adhere to ethical guidelines to ensure that their visuals are accurate, transparent, and free from deception. Here are key considerations for avoiding misleading visuals:

1. Accuracy and Truthfulness:

- Visuals should accurately represent the information they convey. Distorting data or presenting false information is unethical.

- Avoid cropping or altering images in a way that changes their context or meaning.

2. Contextual Clarity:

- Ensure that visuals are presented in a clear and appropriate context. Ambiguity can lead to misinterpretation.

- Provide context and explanations when necessary to help viewers understand the visuals correctly.

3. Data Presentation:

- Represent data accurately and honestly. Choose appropriate scales, axes, and labeling to prevent misrepresentation.

- Avoid selective data omission or manipulation to support a particular narrative.

4. Authenticity:

- Use authentic and unaltered visuals whenever possible. Avoid using staged or manipulated images that mislead viewers.

- Clearly distinguish between real and digitally generated content when applicable.

5. Attribution and Sources:

- Always attribute visuals to their original sources and provide proper citations when using third-party content.

- Verify the credibility and reliability of the sources to avoid disseminating false information.

6. Visual Metaphors and Symbols:

- Be cautious when using metaphors and symbols in visuals. Ensure they are not misleading or open to misinterpretation.

- Consider how viewers from different cultural backgrounds might perceive visual metaphors.

7. Avoiding Exaggeration:

- Refrain from exaggerating aspects of visuals for dramatic effect or sensationalism. It can mislead viewers and compromise trust.

8. Transparency:

- Clearly disclose any enhancements, manipulations, or retouching applied to visuals. Transparency is crucial in maintaining credibility.

9. Fact-Checking:

- Conduct thorough fact-checking and verification of data and visuals before publication.

- Correct any inaccuracies promptly if they are discovered after publication.

10. Ethical Guidelines: - Adhere to ethical guidelines and industry standards in visual communication. Organizations and associations often provide ethical frameworks for designers to follow.

Avoiding misleading visuals is not only a matter of professional ethics but also a way to uphold the integrity of visual communication. By ensuring that visuals accurately represent the intended message and are presented transparently, visual communicators can build trust with their audiences and contribute to responsible and ethical communication practices.

In the following section, we will explore real-world case studies that delve into ethical dilemmas related to visual communication, providing insights into the complexities of ethical decision-making in the field.

Case Studies in Ethical Dilemmas

Examining real-world case studies is an effective way to understand the ethical challenges that can arise in visual communication. These case studies shed light on complex situations where ethical considerations played a pivotal role in decision-making. Let's explore some illustrative examples:

1. Photojournalism and Image Manipulation:

Scenario: A photojournalist covering a protest captures a powerful image of a demonstrator facing off with police. The photo is compelling, but the journalist is tempted to enhance the image's dramatic effect by altering the colors and contrast.

Ethical Dilemma: Should the photojournalist alter the image to make it more impactful, or should they adhere to the principles of journalistic integrity, which prohibit significant image manipulation?

2. Advertising and Body Image:

Scenario: An advertising agency is tasked with promoting a fashion brand's new collection. The agency uses Photoshop to extensively retouch the models in the campaign, creating unrealistic body proportions and flawless skin.

Ethical Dilemma: Is it ethical for the advertising agency to perpetuate unrealistic beauty standards by digitally altering the appearance of models, potentially contributing to body image issues among consumers?

3. Data Visualization and Simplification:

Scenario: A data visualization designer is tasked with creating a chart for a research report. The data shows a subtle but statistically significant trend, which the designer exaggerates in the chart to make it more visually apparent.

Ethical Dilemma: Does the designer have an ethical responsibility to accurately represent the data, even if it means the trend is less noticeable, or is it acceptable to enhance the visual impact of the chart at the risk of misrepresenting the data?

4. Environmental Advocacy and Image Selection:

Scenario: An environmental advocacy group is creating a campaign to raise awareness about deforestation. They have a powerful image of a clear-cut forest with fallen trees and wildlife in distress. However, the image was taken in a different location and doesn't represent the specific area they are advocating for.

Ethical Dilemma: Should the advocacy group use the compelling image to elicit an emotional response, even though it may mislead viewers about the exact location and circumstances of deforestation?

5. User Interface Design and Dark Patterns:

Scenario: A user interface designer is working on an e-commerce website. The designer is pressured to use dark patterns—manipulative design techniques—to encourage users to make purchases or subscribe to services they might not need.

Ethical Dilemma: Is it ethical for the designer to employ dark patterns to boost conversions, even if it means deceiving users or compromising their trust in the brand?

These case studies highlight the ethical complexities that visual communicators often face. Ethical decision-making in visual communication requires careful consideration of principles such as honesty, transparency, integrity, and respect for the audience. It also underscores the importance of adhering to ethical guidelines and industry standards to navigate these dilemmas responsibly.

Chapter 13: Future Trends in Visual Communication

The significance and impact of "Future Trends in Visual Communication" will be profound and far-reaching across various domains and industries. Here's how and where these trends will be important:

1. **Marketing and Advertising:**

- Future trends in visual communication will revolutionize marketing and advertising. AI-driven personalization, AR-powered interactive ads, and immersive VR experiences will engage audiences like never before.

- Sustainability in design will appeal to eco-conscious consumers, making eco-friendly branding a competitive advantage.

2. **Education and Training:**

- Visual communication trends, particularly in VR and AR, will transform education. Virtual classrooms, realistic simulations, and interactive educational content will enhance learning experiences.

- Educators can use AI to personalize teaching materials and adapt to individual student needs.

3. **Healthcare and Medicine:**

- VR and AR will be vital tools for medical training, surgery simulations, and patient education. Visual communication will help convey complex medical information in a more understandable and engaging way.

- Machine learning will aid in medical image analysis, diagnostics, and treatment recommendations.

4. **Design and Architecture:**

- Architects and designers will use VR for immersive walkthroughs of buildings and spaces. This will aid in design refinement and client presentations.

- 3D printing and holography will enable designers to create physical prototypes and interactive design displays.

5. **Gaming and Entertainment:**

- VR will be the future of gaming, offering unparalleled immersion and interactive experiences.

- The entertainment industry will use holography for live events and performances, creating visually stunning shows.

6. **Environmental Conservation:**

- Sustainability in design will play a crucial role in raising awareness about environmental issues.

Visual communication will be a powerful tool for environmental advocacy.

- Eco-friendly materials and energy-efficient visuals will contribute to reducing the carbon footprint of design projects.

7. **Business and Industry:**

- AI-driven data visualization and analytics will aid businesses in making data-driven decisions.

- Sustainable design practices will align with corporate social responsibility goals and enhance brand reputation.

8. **User Experience (UX) and User Interface (UI) Design:**

- UX/UI designers will need to adapt to the unique challenges of designing for VR and AR interfaces.

- AI-driven chatbots and virtual assistants will improve user interactions.

9. **Media and Journalism:**

- AI will assist in content creation, fact-checking, and personalized news delivery.

- VR and AR will enable immersive journalism experiences, allowing audiences to step into news stories.

10. **Ethics and Responsibility:**

- Ethical considerations will become even more critical as technology advances. Visual communicators will need to navigate complex ethical dilemmas.

- The responsible use of AI and data in visuals will be essential to maintain trust and transparency.

In summary, future trends in visual communication will be transformative across a wide range of fields and applications. They will enhance engagement, improve learning, drive innovation, and contribute to a more sustainable and ethical future. Professionals in visual communication will play a pivotal role in harnessing these trends to create impactful and responsible visual content.

Emerging Technologies

Emerging technologies are at the forefront of innovation in the field of visual communication. They are revolutionizing how visuals are created, consumed, and interacted with. Here's a detailed look at the significance of emerging technologies in visual communication:

1. Artificial Intelligence (AI):

- **Automated Content Creation:** AI-powered tools can generate visuals, including images, videos, and graphics, based on text inputs. This streamlines content creation for designers and marketers.

- **Personalization:** AI algorithms analyze user data to tailor visuals and messages for specific audiences. This enhances engagement and conversion rates by delivering content relevant to individual preferences.

- **Data Visualization:** AI can transform complex data into easily digestible visual formats, making it accessible to a broader audience.

2. Augmented Reality (AR) and Virtual Reality (VR):

- **Immersive Experiences:** AR overlays digital information onto the real world, while VR creates entirely immersive digital environments. These technologies are used in marketing, training, education, and entertainment to engage users on a deeper level.

- **Interactive Storytelling:** VR enables storytellers to immerse audiences in narratives, creating powerful and memorable experiences.

- **Product Visualization:** AR allows consumers to virtually try products before purchasing, improving the shopping experience.

3. Machine Learning:

- **Visual Recognition:** Machine learning algorithms can analyze images and videos, recognizing objects, faces, and patterns. This has applications in content moderation, image tagging, and security.

- **Recommendation Systems:** ML-powered recommendation engines use visual data to suggest products, content, or experiences tailored to individual preferences.

4. 3D Printing:

- **Prototyping and Production:** 3D printing is not only revolutionizing manufacturing but also visual communication. Designers can create physical prototypes, architectural models, and interactive displays.

- **Customization:** Personalized 3D-printed visuals and products are becoming more accessible, allowing for unique and tailored designs.

5. Holography:

- **3D Visualizations:** Holographic displays provide 3D visuals without the need for special glasses.

They are used in presentations, product showcases, and entertainment, offering an immersive experience.

- **Telepresence:** Holographic telepresence allows remote participants to appear as lifelike holograms in meetings and events.

6. Challenges and Considerations:

- **Ethical Implications:** Emerging technologies raise ethical questions about data privacy, misinformation, and deepfake visuals. Visual communicators must navigate these challenges responsibly.

- **User Experience (UX):** Designing for emerging technologies like VR and AR requires a deep understanding of user experience and interaction design. Ensuring user comfort and minimizing motion sickness is crucial.

- **Accessibility:** Visual communicators need to ensure that emerging technologies are inclusive and accessible to individuals with disabilities.

- **Environmental Impact:** As these technologies advance, their environmental impact should be considered, with an emphasis on sustainability and responsible design practices.

Incorporating these emerging technologies into visual communication offers exciting opportunities for creativity, engagement, and innovation. However, it also comes with the responsibility to navigate ethical, accessibility, and environmental considerations to ensure that these technologies are harnessed for the betterment of society.

Visual Communication in Virtual Reality

Virtual Reality (VR) is a transformative technology that has a profound impact on visual communication. It offers immersive, three-dimensional experiences that engage users in ways that traditional media cannot. Let's explore the importance and applications of visual communication in VR in more detail:

1. Immersive Storytelling:

- VR enables storytellers to immerse audiences in narratives. Instead of passive observation, users become active participants in the story, creating a deeper emotional connection.

- Storytelling in VR can take various forms, from cinematic experiences to interactive narratives where users make choices that affect the storyline.

2. Education and Training:

- VR provides a dynamic platform for education and training. It allows learners to explore complex concepts, historical settings, or intricate machinery in a realistic, hands-on manner.

- Medical students can practice surgeries, pilots can simulate flight scenarios, and engineers can interact with 3D models of machinery.

3. Architectural Visualization:

- Architects and designers use VR to visualize building designs in three-dimensional space. This enables clients and stakeholders to experience a building before construction begins, facilitating better decision-making.

- Users can virtually walk through architectural models, examining every detail and gaining a realistic sense of scale and proportion.

4. Product Visualization:

- E-commerce and retail industries use VR for product visualization. Customers can virtually try on clothing, view furniture in their own living spaces, or examine products in 3D detail before making purchasing decisions.

- This enhances the shopping experience, reduces return rates, and boosts customer confidence.

5. Gaming and Entertainment:

- VR gaming is a rapidly growing industry. Gamers are transported into immersive virtual worlds where they can interact with environments and characters.

- Entertainment industries are also exploring VR for live concerts, art exhibitions, and immersive experiences.

6. Challenges and Considerations:

- **UX and Interaction Design:** Designing for VR requires a deep understanding of user experience (UX) and interaction design. Ensuring user comfort, minimizing motion sickness, and creating intuitive interfaces are critical.

- **Content Creation:** Creating VR content can be resource-intensive. Designers must consider the development of 3D models, textures, and environments.

- **Accessibility:** Efforts are ongoing to make VR accessible to individuals with disabilities. This includes designing for users with mobility impairments, visual impairments, and hearing impairments.

7. Future Opportunities:

- The evolution of VR hardware and software continues, offering opportunities for even more realistic and interactive experiences.

- Collaboration and social interaction in VR are areas with vast potential, allowing users to meet, work, and socialize in virtual spaces.

Visual communication in VR is an exciting frontier that provides unique opportunities for engagement and interaction. It enhances storytelling, education, design, and entertainment, while also presenting challenges related to UX, content creation, and accessibility. As VR technology evolves, its applications in visual communication are expected to expand, providing new ways to captivate and inform audiences.

Sustainability in Design

Sustainability in design is a growing imperative in visual communication. It encompasses practices, principles, and considerations aimed at reducing the environmental impact of design processes and promoting ethical, eco-friendly design choices. Here's a deeper look into the importance and applications of sustainability in visual communication:

1. Eco-Friendly Materials:

- **Recycled and Upcycled Materials:** Designers are increasingly turning to recycled and upcycled materials for their projects. These materials reduce waste, conserve resources, and often come with unique textures and aesthetics.

- **Renewable Materials:** Sustainable design prioritizes materials that are renewable and environmentally friendly. Bamboo, cork, and organic textiles are examples of materials that can be used in visual communication.

2. Energy Efficiency:

- **Energy-Efficient Printing:** Sustainable design practices involve energy-efficient printing methods. For example, using digital printing over offset printing can reduce energy consumption.

- **LED Displays:** LED technology is energy-efficient and is widely used in signage and displays. LED screens consume less power compared to traditional fluorescent lighting.

3. Minimalism:

- **Simplification:** Minimalist design principles emphasize simplicity and the removal of unnecessary elements. By eliminating visual clutter, designers not only achieve a clean and elegant aesthetic but also reduce the environmental impact of excess production.

- **Resource Efficiency**: Minimalist design often means using fewer resources, whether it's ink, paper, or other materials. This translates to reduced waste and lower environmental footprint.

4. Ethical Consumption:

- **Promoting Sustainable Products:** Visual communication can play a significant role in promoting sustainable products and practices. Sustainable branding and marketing campaigns highlight eco-friendly products, ethical sourcing, and responsible manufacturing.

- **Environmental Awareness:** Designers can create visuals that raise awareness about environmental issues, such as deforestation, climate change, or pollution, driving positive action and behavioral change.

5. Environmental Impact Assessment:

- **Carbon Footprint Analysis:** Sustainability in design involves assessing the carbon footprint of design projects. Designers evaluate the energy consumption, emissions, and waste generation associated with their work.

- **Life Cycle Analysis:** Understanding the environmental impact of a design's entire life cycle, from production to disposal, helps identify areas for improvement.

6. Responsible Packaging:

- **Reducing Packaging Waste:** Sustainable packaging design seeks to minimize waste by using eco-friendly materials, reducing excess packaging, and designing for easy recycling.

- **Reuse and Upcycling:** Designers can create packaging that encourages reuse or repurposing, contributing to a circular economy.

7. Advocacy and Education:

- **Visual Campaigns:** Visual communication can be a powerful tool for advocacy. Campaigns, posters, and visuals raise awareness about sustainability issues and inspire action.

- **Educational Content:** Sustainable design can be integrated into educational materials, teaching future designers and consumers about eco-conscious choices.

As environmental concerns continue to grow, sustainability in design is not only a responsible ethical choice but also a strategic one. Brands that embrace sustainable design practices often resonate with environmentally conscious consumers, strengthen their brand image, and contribute to a greener future. Designers and visual communicators play a crucial role in driving these positive changes by prioritizing sustainability in their work.

Chapter 14: Resources for Visual Communication Professionals

Recommended Tools and Software

In the fast-paced world of visual communication, having the right tools and software at your disposal can make all the difference. In this chapter, we'll explore a curated list of recommended tools and software that are essential for visual communication professionals. These resources span a wide range of applications, from graphic design to video editing, and will help you create stunning visuals and stay at the top of your game.

Graphic Design and Illustration:

1. **Adobe Creative Cloud:** Adobe's suite of creative software, including Photoshop, Illustrator, and InDesign, is the industry standard for graphic design and illustration.

2. **CorelDRAW:** A versatile vector graphic design software that's excellent for logo design and vector illustration.

3. **Canva:** A user-friendly online graphic design tool with a wide array of templates for social media graphics, presentations, and more.

Video Editing and Animation:

4. **Adobe Premiere Pro:** A professional video editing software used by filmmakers, video editors, and content creators for video production.

5. **Final Cut Pro X:** Apple's video editing software known for its intuitive interface and advanced features for Mac users.

6. **After Effects:** Adobe's software for motion graphics and visual effects, essential for creating animations and dynamic visuals.

3D Modeling and Rendering:

7. **Autodesk Maya:** A powerful 3D animation and modeling software used in film, television, and game development.

8. **Blender:** An open-source 3D creation suite suitable for modeling, animation, rendering, and more.

Photography:

9. **Adobe Lightroom:** A photo editing and organization tool for photographers, offering powerful image enhancement features.

10. **Capture One:** Professional-grade photo editing software known for its robust color grading and tethering capabilities.

Web and UX/UI Design:

11. **Sketch:** A design tool tailored for user interface and user experience (UI/UX) designers, popular for creating web and app interfaces.

12. **Figma:** A collaborative design tool that works seamlessly in the cloud, allowing multiple team members to work on the same project simultaneously.

Typography:

13. **Google Fonts:** A vast library of free, open-source fonts that can be easily integrated into web and print projects.

14. **Adobe Fonts:** A collection of high-quality fonts available with an Adobe Creative Cloud subscription.

Project Management and Collaboration:

15. **Trello:** A visual project management tool that helps teams organize tasks and collaborate efficiently.

16. **Asana:** A task and project management platform that streamlines workflows and enhances team communication.

Stock Resources:

17. **Adobe Stock:** A vast collection of royalty-free images, videos, and templates accessible within the Adobe Creative Cloud.

18. **Shutterstock:** A popular source for high-quality stock photos, illustrations, and footage.

These recommended tools and software are essential for visual communication professionals to streamline their work, enhance creativity, and produce visually stunning content. Whether you're a graphic designer, videographer, web designer, or photographer, having access to the right resources is crucial for success in this dynamic field. This chapter will provide you with valuable insights into these tools and how to leverage them effectively to elevate your visual communication projects.

Online Communities and Forums

In the ever-evolving field of visual communication, staying connected with peers, sharing knowledge, and seeking inspiration are vital aspects of professional growth. Online communities and forums provide an invaluable platform for visual communication professionals to interact, learn, and collaborate. Here, we'll explore some of the top online communities and forums where visual communication enthusiasts can connect and thrive:

1. **Behance:** Behance is an Adobe-owned platform that allows designers to showcase their portfolios, share projects, and connect with other creatives worldwide. It's a vibrant community where professionals can gain exposure and inspiration.

2. **Dribbble:** Dribbble is a community of designers, illustrators, and creatives who showcase their work in "shots." It's a place to discover new design trends, get feedback on projects, and connect with potential collaborators.

3. **Reddit - r/Design:** Reddit hosts numerous design-related subreddits, with r/Design being one of the most popular. It's a place to share design work, discuss industry trends, and seek advice from fellow designers.

4. **Designer News:** This online community is dedicated to web and graphic designers. It features discussions on design-related topics, job postings, and a place to share design inspiration.

5. **Adobe Community:** Adobe's official community is a hub for users of Adobe software. It offers support, tutorials, and a space for users to connect and share their experiences with Adobe tools.

6. **LinkedIn Groups:** LinkedIn hosts a variety of professional groups related to visual

communication, graphic design, and related fields. Joining relevant groups can lead to valuable networking opportunities.

7. **CreativeBloq Forum:** CreativeBloq's forum covers a wide range of design topics, including web design, graphic design, and more. It's a space for designers to share insights and discuss industry news.

8. **UX Design Institute Community:** For UX and UI designers, the UX Design Institute Community offers discussions on user experience design, courses, and best practices.

9. **Stack Exchange - Graphic Design:** Stack Exchange's Graphic Design community is a Q&A platform where designers can ask and answer questions on design-related topics.

10. **AIGA Eye on Design:** AIGA's Eye on Design platform includes a blog and an online community. It's a source of design inspiration, industry news, and a place for creatives to connect.

11. **Designer Hangout:** An invite-only community for UX/UI designers, Designer Hangout hosts discussions, webinars, and events focused on user experience design.

12. **Designspiration:** A visual discovery and design platform, Designspiration is an excellent source

for design inspiration and a place to share your own work.

These online communities and forums provide valuable resources for visual communication professionals to expand their knowledge, showcase their work, seek feedback, and connect with like-minded individuals. By actively participating in these platforms, professionals can stay updated on industry trends, collaborate on projects, and find support and inspiration throughout their careers.

Books and Further Reading

In the realm of visual communication, the importance of continuous learning and staying updated with industry trends cannot be overstated. Books serve as invaluable resources for deepening your knowledge, honing your skills, and gaining fresh perspectives. Here's a selection of essential books and further reading materials for visual communication professionals:

Graphic Design and Typography:

1. **"Thinking with Type" by Ellen Lupton:** This typography classic explores the art and science of typography, offering insights into type design and layout principles.

2. **"Logo Design Love" by David Airey:** A comprehensive guide to logo design, this book delves into the process of creating memorable and effective logos.

3. **"Grid Systems in Graphic Design" by Josef Müller-Brockmann:** An exploration of grid-based design, this book is a must-read for designers seeking to create structured and visually pleasing layouts.

Web and UX/UI Design:

4. **"Don't Make Me Think" by Steve Krug:** A usability expert's guide to web design, this book emphasizes user-friendly design principles and practices.

5. **"The Elements of User Experience" by Jesse James Garrett:** An essential read for UX professionals, it outlines the elements and processes involved in creating a compelling user experience.

6. **"Mobile First" by Luke Wroblewski:** With the rise of mobile devices, this book provides insights into designing for smaller screens and mobile user behavior.

Data Visualization and Infographics:

7. **"The Visual Display of Quantitative Information" by Edward R. Tufte:** A seminal work

on data visualization, it explores the principles of presenting data effectively.

8. **"Information Graphics" by Sandra Rendgen:** A beautifully illustrated book showcasing innovative and informative information graphics.

9. **"Good Charts" by Scott Berinato:** Learn how to create impactful charts and visualizations that convey complex information clearly.

Photography and Image Editing:

10. **"The Photographer's Eye" by Michael Freeman:** This book explores the principles of composition and visual storytelling in photography.

11. **"Adobe Photoshop Classroom in a Book" by Adobe Creative Team:** For Photoshop enthusiasts, this official guide covers essential techniques for image editing and manipulation.

12. **"Light Science and Magic" by Fil Hunter, Steven Biver, and Paul Fuqua:** A comprehensive guide to understanding the physics of light and how it affects photography.

Visual Communication Theory and Practice:

13. **"Visual Communication: Images with Messages" by Paul Martin Lester:** This book delves into the theory and history of visual communication, exploring how images convey messages.

14. **"The Design of Everyday Things" by Don Norman:** A thought-provoking read on design psychology, usability, and the impact of design on everyday life.

15. **"Show and Tell: How Everybody Can Make Extraordinary Presentations" by Dan Roam:** Learn the art of visual storytelling and effective communication through visuals.

These books encompass a wide range of topics within visual communication, from graphic design and typography to web design, UX/UI design, data visualization, and photography. Whether you're a seasoned professional or just starting your journey in the field, these resources offer valuable insights and practical knowledge to enhance your skills and creativity. Reading and continuous learning are key to staying at the forefront of visual communication in an ever-evolving digital landscape.

Appendix:
Glossary of Visual Communication Terms

Visual communication encompasses a wide range of concepts, techniques, and terminology. This glossary serves as a quick reference guide to help you navigate the terminology used in the field of visual communication:

A

- **Alignment:** The arrangement of elements along a common axis, creating order and cohesion in a design.

- **Aspect Ratio:** The proportion of an image or screen's width to its height, often expressed as a ratio (e.g., 16:9).

- **Aesthetics:** The study of beauty and artistic principles, often applied to design to enhance visual appeal.

B

- **Balance:** The distribution of visual weight in a design, ensuring equilibrium and harmony.

- **Branding:** The process of creating a unique visual identity and message for a product, service, or organization.

C

- **Contrast:** The difference in visual properties (e.g., color, size, shape) that create visual interest and separation.

- **Color Theory:** The study of color and its interactions, including concepts like the color wheel, complementary colors, and color harmony.

- **Composition:** The arrangement of visual elements in a design, including the use of space, balance, and hierarchy.

D

- **DPI (Dots Per Inch):** A measure of the resolution of an image, indicating the number of dots (pixels) in one inch.

- **Typography:** The art and technique of arranging type, including fonts, spacing, and text layout.

E

- **Emphasis:** The visual emphasis placed on a specific element to draw attention and create focal points.

F

- **Focal Point:** The area in a design that captures the viewer's attention and is often the most important element.

- **Flat Design:** A design style characterized by minimalistic and two-dimensional elements, emphasizing simplicity and clarity.

G

- **Grid:** A framework of evenly spaced horizontal and vertical lines used for alignment and organization in design.

H

- **Hierarchy:** The organization of elements to convey their relative importance and guide the viewer's eye.

I

- **Iconography:** The use of symbols and icons to convey ideas, concepts, or actions in a visual form.

- **Infographic:** A visual representation of information or data, often using charts, graphs, and illustrations to simplify complex concepts.

L

- **Layout:** The arrangement of visual elements on a page, screen, or canvas to create a cohesive design.

M

- **Mockup:** A visual prototype or representation of a design, often used for testing and presentation purposes.

P

- **Pixel:** The smallest unit of a digital image, representing a single point of color.

R

- **Resolution:** The level of detail and clarity in an image, often measured in pixels per inch (PPI or DPI).

- **Responsive Design:** Designing digital content to adapt and display optimally on various devices and screen sizes.

S

- **Saturation:** The intensity or purity of a color, with high saturation being vibrant and low saturation appearing muted.

- **Typography:** The art and technique of arranging type, including fonts, spacing, and text layout.

U

- **User Experience (UX):** The overall experience and satisfaction a user has when interacting with a product, website, or application.

- **User Interface (UI):** The visual elements and design of an application or website that users interact with.

V

- **Vector Graphics:** Graphics created using mathematical equations, allowing for scalability without loss of quality.

- **Visual Hierarchy:** The arrangement of visual elements to guide the viewer's eye and prioritize information.

W

- **Whitespace:** The empty or unmarked space in a design, used for visual separation and clarity.

This glossary provides a foundation for understanding the terminology commonly used in visual communication. As the field continues to evolve, new terms and concepts may emerge, making ongoing learning and exploration essential for professionals in this dynamic discipline.

Recommended Books

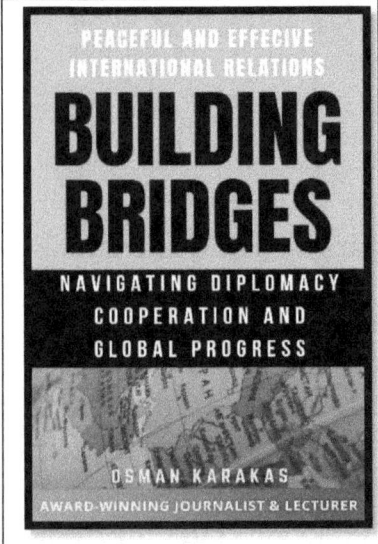

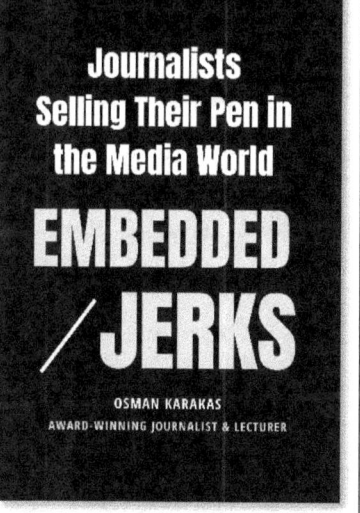

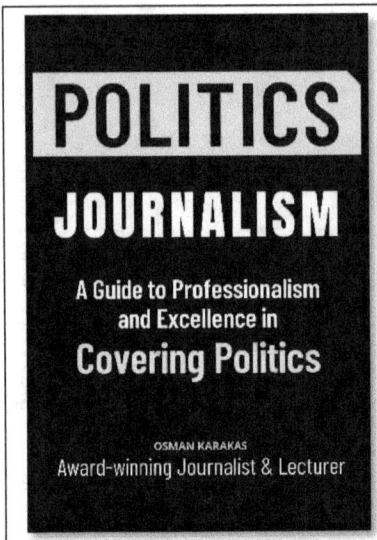

The collection of books is accessible for purchase on Amazon.com platform.

www.ingramcontent.com/pod-product-compliance
Lightning Source LLC
Chambersburg PA
CBHW072148290526
45794CB00004B/1448